TEEN
ANXIETY

of related interest

Starving the Anxiety Gremlin
A Cognitive Behavioural Therapy Workbook on Anxiety Management for Young People
Kate Collins-Donnelly
ISBN 978 1 84905 341 9
eISBN 978 0 85700 673 8

Helping Adolescents and Adults to Build Self-Esteem
A Photocopiable Resource Book
2nd edition
Deborah M. Plummer
ISBN 978 1 84905 425 6
eISBN 978 0 85700 794 0

Adolescent Volcanoes
Helping Adolescents and their Parents to Deal with Anger
Warwick Pudney and Éliane Whitehouse
Foreword by Professor Max Abbott
ISBN 978 1 84905 218 4
eISBN 978 0 85700 596 0

Building Happiness, Resilience and Motivation in Adolescents
A Positive Psychology Curriculum for Well-Being
Ruth MacConville and Tina Rae
ISBN 978 1 84905 261 0
eISBN 978 0 85700 548 9

The KidsKope Peer Mentoring Programme
A Therapeutic Approach to Help Children and
Young People Build Resilience and Deal with Conflict
Nina Wroe and Penny McFarlane
ISBN 978 1 84905 500 0
eISBN 978 0 85700 903 6

TEEN ANXIETY

A CBT and ACT Activity Resource Book
for Helping Anxious Adolescents

RAYCHELLE CASSADA LOHMANN

Jessica Kingsley *Publishers*
London and Philadelphia

First published in 2015
by Jessica Kingsley Publishers
73 Collier Street
London N1 9BE, UK
and
400 Market Street, Suite 400
Philadelphia, PA 19106, USA

www.jkp.com

Library of Congress Cataloging in Publication Data
A CIP catalog record for this book is available from the Library of Congress

British Library Cataloguing in Publication Data
A CIP catalogue record for this book is available from the British Library

ISBN 978 1 84905 969 5
eISBN 978 0 85700 859 6

Printed and bound in Great Britain

The Serenity Prayer

God grant me the serenity
to accept the things I cannot change;
courage to change the things I can;
and wisdom to know the difference.

CONTENTS

LETTER TO A PROFESSIONAL

Dear Fellow Colleague

Thank you for investing in *Teen Anxiety*, an adolescent anxiety management program written especially for you with the anxious teen in mind. This book uses a unique approach offering both practical and relevant techniques and exercises to help teens cope more effectively with anxiety. It is a one-of-a-kind professional guide offering a step-by-step approach which uses Cognitive Behavioral Therapy (CBT) and Acceptance Commitment Therapy (ACT) as the crux of the program.

Anxiety is a growing problem affecting teens. It is estimated that more than 10 percent of today's teens are diagnosed with an anxiety disorder and only a few of those get the treatment that they need. That's a lot of young people. Why are teens susceptible to high levels of anxiety? To answer this question you just have to look at all of the stressors in a teen's life. From friendships to studies/school to parents/family to home/environmental pressures, teens are in a constant struggle to find balance in their lives. Unfortunately, many teens are ill-equipped to handle everything that life throws at them and they reach their breaking point.

When stress becomes excessive and unbearable it can lead to something more serious… *anxiety*. Anxiety carries its own host of problems that can have an adverse impact on the teen's life. It can lead to avoidance, panic, sleep problems, self-medication, and even self-harm. According to the Partnership for a Drug-Free America (2008), 73 percent of teenagers reported that stress was the primary reason for drug use. When teens turn to substances to help them cope with life, then we have a huge problem on our hands.

It is not uncommon for teens to struggle with anxiety as they are encountering life's developmental, physical, emotional, and psychological changes. Teens are faced with so many complex and potentially life-altering decisions. One decision, made in a matter of seconds, can change the course of their life. When you think about it in these terms, it's no wonder anxiety levels are at an all time high.

Teens who struggle with anxiety often feel vulnerable and helpless. They don't like feeling anxious, but they don't know how to make the feeling stop. They may feel as though they are stuck with this persistent and unbearable emotion. The good news is that anxiety is controllable and treatable. With the assistance of this guidebook and therapy, teens can learn to stand strong in the face of anxiety and overcome the power it has on their life.

Teen Anxiety is designed as a practical tool to help you help your adolescent clients cope with their anxious feelings. There are more than 50 skill-based activities in this book that are grounded in CBT and ACT. CBT is one of today's most respected anxiety therapeutic approaches; its effectiveness has been well documented in the literature.

While ACT is a relatively new therapeutic approach, it is producing some very promising results in respect to anxiety. ACT falls under the same umbrella as CBT, but places the emphasis on emotional acceptance, psychological flexibility, and mindfulness, rather than changing thoughts. Both approaches allow your clients the opportunity to experience the best that the psychological field has to offer.

The CBT and ACT techniques taught in this workbook will help teens reflect, become more mindful of their surroundings and feelings, change/accept their thoughts and reactions to anxiety, and ultimately conquer their anxiety.

Teen Anxiety will help your clients:

- identify their values

- set goals congruent with these values

- identify maladaptive schemas

- accept thoughts and feelings for what they are rather than fight them

- live in the "here and now" by becoming more mindfully aware of how they are thinking, feeling, and behaving

- increase cognitive flexibility.

Your commitment and dedication to working with these teens will play an important role in the treatment of this paralyzing and sometimes debilitating emotion. With the right treatment regimen adolescents can effectively learn how to manage anxiety and live a more meaningful and fulfilling life. Caring and dedicated professionals, such as you, can have a positive impact and make a significant difference in the life of an anxious teen.

Sincerely,

Raychelle Cassada Lohmann

MAKING THE MOST
OF THIS BOOK

As a mental health professional it can be difficult to help anxious teens face their fear and anxiety. A client-centered treatment manual, such as *Teen Anxiety*, provides structure that extends beyond the scope of the treatment session. To gain the maximum benefits of this workbook, please review the layout and suggestions of how to incorporate *Teen Anxiety* in your client's treatment plan.

The book's layout

Before exploring the layout and contents of this book any further there are a few things to note. First, the words "therapist" and "clinician" are used interchangeably throughout this book. Second, this book is not a cookbook to use as a substitute for treating and managing anxiety, but rather a resource and guide to assist you in developing the most comprehensive and efficient treatment plan. Third, this book is written for the adolescent stage of development. It can serve a variety of therapeutic purposes, for example using the book as a group curriculum or assigning the activities as homework. Homework is a wonderful counseling tool. It can be extremely beneficial in generalizing skills and techniques taught in session to the client's life.

Teen Anxiety is divided into three distinct parts described below.

Part I

Part I covers the nuts and bolts of anxiety, from the clinical definition and symptomology to the cutting edge of clinical and empirical data that show what works in treating this often debilitating condition. Also covered in Part I are the unique components and therapeutic techniques such as Cognitive Behavioral Therapy (CBT) and Acceptance Commitment Therapy (ACT). This section offers a brief review of both therapeutic approaches as well as unifying them to achieve the most effective therapeutic gains. Finally, the diagnostic criteria of Anxiety Disorder, according to the newest version of the *Diagnostic and Statistical Manual of Mental Disorders* (DSM-5) (American Psychiatric Association 2013), is reviewed as well as other diagnostic conditions covered in this guidebook.

Part II

Part II is the most extensive part of this workbook: the adolescent activities. This part of the book explores anxiety from a social and emotional, physiological, and intellectual (cognitive) perspective. The activities sections are laid out in a step-by-step progression of chapters and are organized in the user-friendly format.

Chapter-by-chapter

To make this manual user-friendly, each chapter follows the same format. The format is as follows:

- Introductory section about the topics covered.

- Outline of activities that will be covered in the chapter.

- Scaling questions to serve as a pre- and post-anxiety profile assessment to help gauge where your client is currently and how he/she is progressing through the skills and techniques being taught.

- A graph to allow you to chart your client's progress. As your clients work through the *Teen Anxiety* activities it is important to chart their progress. Not only will this be an accountability tool, but it will also help you look at the weaknesses, strengths, growth, and stagnation your clients go through during therapy. This information will help you to adapt and modify your treatment plan.

Scaling questions help with anxious teens

Scaling questions are useful tools to help your clients process growth and change in a non-confrontational way. These questions help clients assess personal situations and track their progress. Scaling questions begin with the worst-case scenario: "the worst the problem has ever been" (zero) to "the best things could be" (ten, maximum). The client is in charge of rating his/her current position on the scale.

Teens are invited to assess where they are and where they want to end up in each of the seven areas. You can maximize the information by using the suggested follow-up questions in each chapter to get your client to explore how he/she can get to where he/she wants to be (e.g. "What number would be good enough for you on the scale? What would that point on the scale feel like? What would you do differently?"). There are three advantages to using scaling questions. First, they are an assessment instrument and provide you with a measurement of your client's progress. Second, they put the client in control of evaluating his/her progress. Third, they are a powerful intervention that assesses whether things get better, stay the same, or get worse.

Using the activities

There are eight to ten activities in each chapter that focus on a specific area of skill development. Teens will relate to the activities as they incorporate them into real-life scenarios. Each activity is designed to be fun, engaging, and interactive, and should take between 20 and 30 minutes to complete.

Each activity has the three basic parts reviewed below:

(i) *Introduction to the skill*

⇌ *Directions to incorporate the skill into practice*

⟷ *Expand on it to encourage additional practice in applying the new skill.*

Incorporating Teen Anxiety *in your practice*

Some examples of how to incorporate *Teen Anxiety* into therapy are highlighted below:

- Use as a part of your in-session treatment.

- Use the activities as the structure guiding your session and assign the follow-up section, *Expand on it* as homework. If using *Teen Anxiety* as a guide in your session, be sure to review the activity prior to the appointment, as many activities require additional materials to complete.

- Use *Teen Anxiety* as a supplemental companion to the treatment plan and assign various activities as homework. To prevent client fatigue it is not recommended to assign one activity a day. Rather, four or five activities in a seven-day span work better. Doing too much too quickly can be counterproductive, and may end up inducing more anxiety. Finding the right pace is an important step in therapy.

- Use the activities as part of a group curriculum. *Teen Anxiety* can be easily adapted and modified to suit a group format. The activities are engaging and could promote an open dialogue with group members. The *Expand on it* section could be used as homework following the group meeting, as it would help reinforce techniques taught in the group independently.

- Use the activities as a part of family therapy. Many of the activities can be done in conjunction with other family members. The activities are non-confrontational and interactive. If you choose, you can incorporate an applicable activity into your work with the family unit.

Part III

Part III is the grand finale! It begins with a brief conclusion and then progresses to one of the most important components of the guide—*Charting progress*. Use the information from the scaling questions and plot them on the chart. The graph will be a visual representation of your client's growth. It is recommended that you chart your client's pre-/post-scaling scores at the completion of each chapter. This approach will save time in the long run.

Many manuals overlook the accountability portion of client success. Use Part III throughout therapy as a resource to help you guide and adjust your treatment plan. The charting section is a wonderful tool to show clients, parents, and other approved treatment providers the growth and progress your client has made throughout therapy. You can even collect data with other clients you are working with to see what's working and what's not working so well. Reviewing this data will help you design the best individualized treatment plan for your client.

Additionally, there is a pre-assessment profile (Activity 1.5) in Chapter 1 and post-assessment profile (Activity 7.9) Chapter 7. Your clients can work through these assessments to do a side-by-side comparison at the end of therapy. This will enable you to see the specific steps of progression they have made on their anxiety management journey.

The final section of Part III includes references and resources. Use this information to broaden your knowledge and understanding of anxiety management, ACT, and CBT.

Part I

CLINICIAN'S GUIDE

Introduction

Childhood should be a time of feeling carefree and happy, but unfortunately for many children, especially the anxious ones, this isn't the case. Children with anxiety are known to suffer in silence (Chansky 2004). They may appear quiet, shy, or reserved, but inside the facade is a racing mind that is inundated with anxious thoughts. Many who suffer from anxiety become prisoners of their fears and insecurities and they desperately need our help.

Anxiety will not dissipate: rather, it will continue to manifest into more severe conditions such as depression, relationship problems and potentially substance abuse in later adulthood (Low *et al.* 2012; Reynolds *et al.* 2013; Saavedra *et al.* 2010). However, if it is detected at early onset, children with anxiety can learn effective coping skills. Most importantly, they can live a happy and productive life without the struggle of anxiety (Rickwood and Bradford 2012).

Anxiety disorders are the most common mental health disorder among young people today. It is estimated that approximately 10 percent of young people aged 13–18 have a diagnosable anxiety disorder, with the average age of onset prior to adolescence (Low *et al.* 2012; Swain *et al.* 2013). Anxiety can significantly impact an individual's social functioning, academic performance, and cognitive development. If left untreated, anxiety manifestations can follow into adulthood, leading to other functioning impairments. It is imperative that anxiety is detected early and that effective interventions are put in place to help teens cope with this debilitating disorder.

About anxiety

Anxiety is defined as an intense emotional state that occurs when one cannot predict the outcome of a situation or guarantee that it will be the desired one (Chansky 2004). Anxiety becomes problematic and is characterized as a disorder when a child exaggerates risks and underestimates the ability to cope in a situation.

Anxiety disorders make up a large number of mental disorders. According to the DSM-5 (American Psychiatric Association 2013) these disorders include:

- Separation Anxiety Disorder

- Selective Mutism

- Specific Phobia

- Social Anxiety Disorder (Social Phobia)

- Panic Disorder

- Panic Attack (Specifier)

- Agoraphobia

- Generalized Anxiety Disorder

- Substance/Medication-Induced Anxiety Disorder

- Anxiety Disorder Due to Another Medical Condition

- Other Specified Anxiety Disorder

- Unspecified Anxiety Disorder.

These disorders are characterized by symptoms of intrusive and disturbing thoughts and experiences, often coupled with physiological symptoms.

Due to the fact that the teen years stand apart from any other stage of life, it's important for those working with this age group to recognize that anxiety may manifest itself differently in adolescence. For example, it's not uncommon for anxious teens to appear shy, to avoid pleasurable activities, or to steer away from social places. They may also pull away from family and friends, although it is not necessarily the people they are avoiding, it is the anxiety. They may absolutely refuse to try anything new as it may make them anxious. Worse still, they may engage in risk-taking behaviors such as self-medication (e.g. drug experimentation), promiscuity, and self-injurious behaviors (Reynolds *et al.* 2013). When anxiety symptoms become unbearable many teens will do anything to alleviate their suffering.

Understanding anxiety

Anxiety is a displeasing but normal emotion that we have all experienced. It becomes activated when we feel frightened, stressed, or threatened and perceive an event as unavoidable or uncontrollable. While anxiety doesn't feel good to us it does serve a purpose—to protect us from danger. Unfortunately, we have become over-sensitized to life stressors, and an emotion that was meant to protect us has now become one that is detrimental to our well-being.

Anxiety can be an all-consuming emotion and it affects our thoughts, our body (e.g. sweating, rapid heartbeat, face flushing, etc.) our feelings, and even our behavior.

When people think about anxiety the following words often come to mind:

- apprehension
- concern
- fear
- impatience
- nervousness
- panic
- restlessness
- stress
- uneasiness
- worry.

The mind is a powerful tool and our body is designed to work in unison with it, so when something isn't right all systems begin working to correct the problem. This is an important thing to keep in mind as we delve into an anxious teen's life. Equally important is understanding that anxiety is not the culprit, but rather a protection mechanism that's been activated so much that a perceived threat and a real threat are indistinguishable.

Anxiety symptoms

Teen anxiety typically involves physical and developmental changes in the teen's body; for example, teens can become overly concerned about how they look, whether people will like them, what others think about them, or whether they are smart or not. You get the picture; teens can become overwhelmed by things that no longer concern many adults. Teens also place a great deal of importance on relationships. Often you'll find that their anxiety is centered on their social interactions and perception of what others think of them. The teen years are also centered on the fight for independence. It's not uncommon for conflict to occur at home when a teen is set on showing that he/she is all grown up.

Anxiety usually includes excessive fear, stress, worry, and restlessness. Anxious teens may be easily agitated, and frustrated and edgy a lot of the time. They may seem to always be on alert, even in the absence of a real threat. Socially, anxious teens may be dependent, needy, and withdrawn. Any stressor may put them on guard and their emotional response may appear out of kilter with the situation. Anxious teens have a tendency to magnify and alter reality, and this can cause problems in their lives.

Along with distorting reality, adolescents who suffer from anxiety on a regular basis experience a variety of physical symptoms. Some of these include muscle tension, stomach ache, headache, back pain, and fatigue. These teens may experience nervous rashes, skin breakouts, frequent perspirations, hyperventilation, nervous shakes, or fidgeting, and they may startle easily. Clearly, the conditions that anxiety brings along with it are far from pleasurable and those who struggle with it are desperate to find relief.

In order to best serve this population, it is important for professionals to stay in tune with adolescent psychological and physiological changes and how anxiety may manifest itself during this stage of development. Below are some common symptoms associated with anxiety.

Behavioral symptoms

- Inability to relax, and/or enjoy life.
- Procrastinating and feeling overwhelmed.
- Running from things that trigger anxiety.
- Inability to concentrate or pay attention.
- Persistently forgetting things and difficulty retaining information.
- Constantly blaming self for unfortunate events.
- Continually needing reassurance and approval.
- Excessively critical of self for making mistakes.
- Mind races repeatedly.

Emotional symptoms

- Persistently feeling apprehensive.

- Constantly worrying about something.

- Chronic impatience.

- Believing the anxiety is uncontrollable and can't be fixed.

- Compulsive thoughts about anxiety-producing events.

- Difficulty stopping anxious thoughts from surfacing.

- Dwelling on the "what ifs."

Physical symptoms

- Muscle tension or body aches.

- Difficulty falling asleep or staying asleep due to an overactive mind.

- Feeling tired all the time.

- Feeling on edge, restless, or nervous.

- Stomach aches, nausea, constipation, or diarrhea.

In order to best help anxious teens it is important to understand what's going on in their body. Developmentally teens are undergoing major changes from social emotional to biological changes to cognitive maturation. The teen body runs the gamut of change.

Developmentally adolescent

Adolescence is a unique and challenging period marked by rapid physical and psychological growth. It is the transitional stage that falls between childhood and adulthood. For many teens it is a difficult stage to navigate through, and for anxious teens it is more difficult as they lack the tools and skills needed to confront this stage.

Emotional and social development

During the adolescent years teens often search for autonomy, identity, and independence (Cromer 2011; Kaufman 2006). As teens search for their identity they may express less affection towards family members, and spend a lot of time with friends. Many teens struggle with dependency on their parents while asserting, their rights to individuality. Aspects such as appearance, social acceptability and fitting in become increasingly important. Emotionally and socially, teens may feel stuck between two stages of development which can lead to identity confusion. Both roles can lead to stress and pressure. According to Kaufman (2006) many people spend their childhood years learning to be like their parents, and their adolescent years learning who they are and how they are different from their parents.

During the adolescent years the following emotional changes may occur:

- Displaying intense emotions. A teen's mood can change sporadically and appear unpredictable. These emotional highs and lows can create increased conflict in a teen's life. The adolescent brain is still maturing and emotional regulation, decision making, and expressing oneself are still developing.

- Displaying sensitivity to others' emotions. Adolescents learn to process communication skills more like an adult. They get better at reading and responding to others' social cues and non-verbal body language. However, these soft skills are still developing so misinterpretation and poor communication frequently occur; when this happens it can wreak havoc in a teen's relationships.

Social development is also crucial for adolescents. Peer relationships are paramount in shaping who and what teens will become. Often peers have more influence on a teen's decisions than his/her own parents do.

During the adolescent years the following emotional changes may occur:

- The quest for finding themselves. Teens are busy trying to figure out who they are and where they fit into the world. This identity search can be influenced by gender, peers, culture, ethnicity, religious beliefs, and family expectations.

- The quest for responsibility. Teens seek to be more adult-like in their decisions and actions. They don't want to be perceived as children any longer, but rather as young adults.

- The quest for experience. The path to adulthood is marked by our experiences, and that's no different for a teen. Teens seek new opportunities and experiences. Some of these experiences may be risky and involve detrimental and life-altering consequences. Over time, most will learn how to control and think through impulsive choices.

- The quest for finding the right thing to do. This is a moral dilemma for many teens. They begin to form who they are apart and in conjunction with their parents' values and morals. It is during this stage of development that most teens learn that they have ownership of their decisions, behaviors, and consequences. Teens will begin to question what they are told to do and what they should do. This is all completely normal in their search to do the right thing.

- The quest for friendship. Friends are strong influencers of teens' decisions. Many teens tap into what their peers think of them in order to gauge their own levels of self-esteem and confidence.

- The quest for a romantic relationship. It is during adolescence that most teens have their first romantic relationship. They are beginning to develop, explore, and even experiment with their sexuality.

- The quest to communicate. The majority of today's teens communicate through the use of electronic devices. While electronic communication is a great way to have a brief conversation or be in the loop of what's going on, it can also be problematic, especially if teens lack communication skills and often misinterpret this abbreviated form of communication. Electronic communication significantly influences teens' interactions with the world in which they live.

Physical development

An adolescent's body undergoes a tremendous amount of change. While each adolescent moves through this stage at different rates, there are some common things that occur, such as puberty. Puberty is defined as the physical and biological changes the body undergoes to reach sexual maturity. By mid-adolescence, if not sooner, most teens' physiological growth is complete; they are at or close to their adult height and weight, and are fully capable of having sex and having their own children (American Academy of Child and Adolescent's Facts for Families 2008; Cromer 2011).

Here are some changes that occur during puberty:

Boys:

- On average, boys begin puberty later than girls.

- Puberty begins between the ages of 9 and 16 years.

- The voice gets deeper.

- Increase in sweating and body odor.

- Acne may form.

- Body and facial hair begin to grow.

- A growth spurt in height happens.

- The growth spurt peaks around the age of 13.5 and slows around 18.

Girls:

- On average, girls begin puberty earlier than boys.

- Puberty begins between the ages of 8 and 14 years.

- Breasts begin to develop.

- Menstruation cycle begins.

- Increase in sweating and body odor.

- Acne may form.

- A growth spurt in height happens as well as widening of the hips.

- The growth spurt peaks around the age of 11.5 and slows around the age of 16.

So aside from teens undergoing social and emotional changes, their bodies are also in transformation. A teen's body is shaping and molding into an adult (American Academy of Child and Adolescent's Facts for Families 2008; Cromer 2011).

Cognitive development

Most teens enter adolescence seeing things as right or wrong, good or bad. They live in the here and now and have a tendency to focus on the present. Teens' present-oriented thinking explains their inability to foresee the long-term consequences of their actions.

Many young teens fall into unrealistic thinking. Below are two types of faulty thinking patterns teens use to justify their behavior:

- "The world is a stage and other people's attention is constantly centered on me. It's all about me, me, me, me, and me." This self-centeredness may seem narcissistic to some and may even appear to border on paranoia, but rest assured it is perfectly normal.

- "It will never happen to me. I am invincible and bad things only happen to other people." This type of thinking may help to explain why teens engage in overly risky and impulsive behavior.

As teens get older it becomes easier for them to set realistic goals for the future. They are also moving from a concrete perspective to the ability to think abstractly and solve more complex problems. Additionally, they are changing from an internal "all about me" view to one that takes into consideration how others feel and think.

Some areas that become more developed in late adolescence are:

- an increase in their interest about their future

- more mature work habits

- an ability to set goals and put a plan in place to reach them

- an increase in emotional regulation

- the ability to think abstractly.

There is a lot of intellectual growth that occurs during this stage of development, but probably one of the most interesting areas of growth is in the development of the brain, particularly in the prefrontal cortex (Casey *et al.* 2011).

Due to the ever-evolving research on adolescents and brain development, this topic is reviewed in more detail to help you better understand and assist your anxious clients.

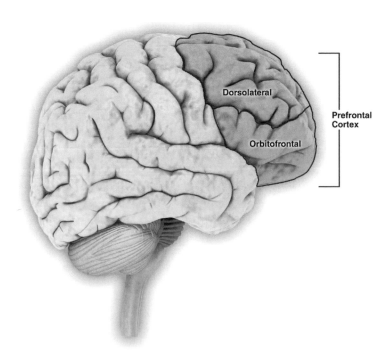

The prefrontal cortex (aka the CEO of the brain) is responsible for problem solving, impulse control, and weighing out options. Unfortunately, for the majority of teens, this area of the brain is not fully developed until the early to mid-twenties. The medial prefrontal cortex (MPC), which is made up of the orbitofrontal cortex (OFC) and anterior cingulate gyrus, is responsible for emotional regulation. A well-developed MPC results in an increase in feeling emotionally balanced (Ridderinkhof *et al.* 2004).

The amygdala, an almond-shaped structure of the prefrontal cortex, has been dubbed the "smoke alarm of the brain." It connects the hypothalamus with other parts of the body, that is the adrenals, which are responsible for the release of stress hormones that activate the fight or flight response. These stress hormones play a role in the maintenance of anxiety. Research has found the amygdala to be hyperresponsive in Post Traumatic Stress Disorder (PTSD) and anxiety disorders (Shin, Rauch, and Pitman 2006). Thus, understanding the role of the amygdala as well as the prefrontal cortex is important in understanding and helping clients process fear and anxiety (Shin, *et al.* 2006).

When these brain connections are not well developed, emotions are not balanced and regulated. A surge of stress hormones may lead to intense anxiety, panic attacks, and physical problems. The overwhelming feeling of anxiety may create an imbalance between the psyche and the mind. The psyche is a psychological term used to describe the entirety of the human mind. It encompasses the unconscious, the conscious, the ego, the human soul/spirit, and the personality. When this imbalance occurs it can cause a person to feel out of control of his/her life. The connection between the body and psyche may lead to an uncanny mixture of emotions, making it feel impossible to regulate and cope with the stressful events.

The role of executive functioning

The most common psychological term for the functions of the prefrontal cortex is *executive functioning*. Executive functioning refers to the cognitive process of an individual's ability to carry out goal-oriented behavior, including impulse control, judgments, self-monitoring, and planning (Casey *et al.* 2011; Pharo *et al.* 2011). Pharo *et al.* (2011) found that personality traits such as impulsivity, sensation seeking, and aggression are related to an increase in reckless behavior. So it appears that brain development does affect behavior. It is believed that there is a link between an individual's personality and the functions of the prefrontal cortex.

According to Pharo *et al.* (2011) the connection between of executive functioning and brain development may hold the key to adolescent risk-taking behavior. Along with risk-taking behavior is the inability for many anxious teens to understand or detect social cues when it comes to aggression. Batanova and Loukas (2011) found that socially anxious youths were more likely to misinterpret social cues in a hostile manner. The underdeveloped teen brain can produce a lot of barriers in therapy.

The two areas of the brain that are most associated with decision making are the amygdala and prefrontal cortex. Casey *et al.* (2011) found that these areas showed more white matter in brain imaging with adolescents who had more emotional difficulties than those who did not. This is supportive of the role of brain development and executive functioning in understanding adolescent anxiety. These regions of the brain are paramount when it comes to decision making, emotional regulation, and inhibitory responses.

Unfortunately, the prefrontal cortex is not fully developed well into the early twenties (Johnson, Blum and Giedd 2009). According to Casey *et al.* (2011) the adolescent years are a period of time when a lot of mental, physical, and hormonal changes are occurring. These changes are often accompanied by an increase in autonomy and an increase in emotional sensitivity (Swartz *et al.* 2014). While many teens emerge from this stage of development unscathed, there are those who do not.

On a promising note, even though the teen brain is developing, teens can still get a lot out of therapy. Just as exercise helps get the body fit and in shape, the brain can also be strengthened through helping teens work through and process thoughts, feelings, and actions. Executive functioning skills can grow stronger through teaching cognitive skills or higher order thinking skills (Pharo *et al.* 2011). Cognitive skills, such as the ones in *Teen Anxiety*, can be taught to help teens practice higher order thinking skills and decrease reckless behavior so the transition into adulthood is a positive one.

Anxiety and parenting

Each child's anxiety is a combination of genetics, temperament, and environmental experiences. Additionally, there is a correlation between anxious children and anxious parents. Anxious parents are seven times more likely to have an anxious child (Chansky 2004). In attempting to gain a greater understanding of a parent's effect on their child's anxiety, it is important to look at the distinct parenting styles that may contribute to the maintenance of anxiety.

Parents play a large role in the development and maintenance of anxiety. Through social modeling, restricting independence, preventing distress, and predicting danger, parents can exacerbate anxiety symptoms in their child. Low *et al.* (2012) found a strong relationship between maternal or paternal mental health history of mood or anxiety disorders and the increased risk of mood or anxiety disorders in offspring. Mood or anxiety disorders are a strong risk factor for the development of these disorders in children of people who have a mood or anxiety disorder. Low *et al.* (2012) highlighted the importance of exploring the relationship of familial clustering of mood or anxiety disorders.

There is also a growing body of evidence that supports a correlation between anxiety disorders and parenting styles (Erozkan 2012; Kendall, Settipani, and Cummings 2012; Kerns *et al.* 2013; Low *et al.* 2012). Overprotective and authoritarian parenting styles appear to be the most dominant with anxious youths (Erozkan 2012). Negative and demanding parenting styles may also act as risk factors for anxiety. Parents of anxious children tend to be anxious, demanding, controlling, display less affection, and be overprotective. Understanding parenting styles in relation to anxiety can help clinicians design a treatment plan to address not only the individual, but also the familial unit.

Adolescents' perception of negative parenting styles also contributes to their level of anxiety. Each of these parenting styles is positively correlated with anxiety: authoritarian, democratic and authoritarian, and protective and demanding. These styles of parenting are related to anxiety sensitivity and adolescents' perception of their ability to handle an anxiety-producing situation (Meuret *et al.* 2012). So, it's important to include parents, if possible, in your therapeutic regimen. Which leads to the next area to be addressed—what therapeutic approach(es) should you use with your anxious clients?

Anxiety and Cognitive Behavioral Therapy

CBT originates with the work of B.F. Skinner (1974), who is known as the father of modern behavior therapy. One of the core beliefs behind CBT is that changing maladaptive thoughts leads to a change in emotions, which results in a change of behavior. There is a large portion of CBT which emphasizes challenging faulty or irrational thoughts rather than resisting them. It is believed that this will decrease self-defeating behavior. Thoughts play a big part in how people feel, which in turn determines the way they act. CBT seeks to identify negative thought patterns and cognitive distortions according to our perception of our surroundings as well as ourselves. The foundation of CBT lies in the belief that our thoughts, not external events, affect the way we feel about and perceive the world around us (Beck 2011).

There are many therapeutic principles associated with CBT, below are some of the most popular:

- CBT is based on an ever-evolving formulation of the client, and the problems he/she experiences are explored in cognitive terms.

- CBT requires a good client—therapist relationship.

- CBT requires collaboration between the therapist and the client.

- CBT is goal-oriented and problem-focused.

- CBT emphasizes the present.

- CBT empowers the client to solve his/her own problems and emphasizes relapse prevention.

- CBT is brief and time-limited.

- CBT sessions are direct and structured.

- CBT teaches patients to identify, evaluate, and respond to their dysfunctional thoughts and beliefs.

- CBT uses various techniques to change thinking, mood, and behavior.

(Beck 1995)

Gatchel and Rollings (2008) define six phases of CBT:

1. assessment

2. reconceptualization

3. skills acquisition

4. skills consolidation and application training

5. generalization and maintenance

6. post-treatment assessment and follow-up.

CBT meets the American Psychological Association's stringent standards of efficacious treatment. In fact, it is often referred to as the "gold standard" for treating anxiety (Podell *et al.* 2013). Youths who participate in CBT therapy show significant reductions in anxiety up to 50–80 percent of the time (Chansky 2004). Many studies have empirically shown that CBT is an effective treatment protocol not only with anxious teens, but also with adults (Aderka *et al.* 2013; Podell *et al.* 2013) Additionally, CBT intervention is an effective way to decrease depression and anxiety in teens (Lusk and Melnyk 2013). CBT offers powerful tools and techniques to help clients confront, challenge, and change anxious thoughts. Exposure techniques are frequently utilized to help clients break stigmatization and overcome fears and phobias. Most importantly, CBT interventions have shown clinical significance in the maintenance of techniques and symptom reduction long after treatment has ended (Arch *et al.* 2012).

Saavedra *et al.* (2010) indicate that research on the effects of CBT on childhood disorders shows very promising results and therapy received in childhood carries forward into young adulthood. CBT has shown effectiveness in treating anxious children and still produces positive results in follow-up studies one year post-treatment (Saavedra *et al.* 2010; Sportel *et al.* 2013).

Although it is an anxiety treatment of choice among many clinicians, there are some shortcomings to CBT. One study reveals that one-third of the children receiving CBT interventions continue to meet the diagnostic criteria for depression and anxiety (Kerns *et al.* 2013). Additionally, research shows that youths with social phobia may be less likely to respond to a CBT treatment program compared with those with other types of anxiety. It appears that while CBT does produce immediate results, the effect diminishes over time. Although CBT still produces overall favorable results in the treatment of anxiety, in relation to social anxiety and social phobia other approaches should be explored, explicitly those approaches that involve more social skills and exposure therapy.

While CBT may have earned the "gold standard" award in the treatment of many psychological disorders, in regards to youth anxiety, about one-third of young people do not respond to it (Podell *et al.* 2013). In fact, CBT's effectiveness has not been well established with Social Anxiety Disorder or Generalized Anxiety Disorder. This has led clinicians to explore other therapeutic means for helping anxious teens. One therapy that is gaining momentum is Acceptance Commitment Therapy, also known as ACT (pronounced "act").

Anxiety and Acceptance Commitment Therapy

Acceptance and Commitment Therapy (ACT) is a behavioral therapy that centralizes around the concepts of acceptance and commitment (Harris 2009; Hayes 2005). ACT can best be understood by the concepts highlighted below:

- **A**ccepting thoughts

- **C**hoosing life directions

- **T**aking action.

Each of these concepts makes ACT a revolutionary form of behavioral and cognitive therapy. One of the things that makes ACT stand apart from CBT is the change of focus. Traditional CBT focuses on changing thoughts in order to alleviate suffering. In contrast, ACT puts attention on feeling and experiencing emotions, rather than fighting them. So, in essence, the goal is not to fight or try to change your thoughts, but rather to recognize what they are and deal with them. The idea is to let go of the struggle to control unwanted thoughts and feelings by being more mindful of the present moment and by committing to actions that are consistent with what you value most in life. In summary, ACT places emphasis on emotional acceptance, psychological flexibility, and mindfulness, rather than on changing thoughts (Harris 2009; Hayes 2005).

The use of ACT in the treatment of anxiety and depression is growing in popularity. Empirical studies are finding that this behavioral therapy is an effective treatment option for a variety of mental health disorders (Sportel *et al.* 2013). One of ACT's core principles is increased psychological flexibility. In fact, Fledderus *et al.* (2013) examined the role of psychological flexibility as a risk factor and change agent in a self-help ACT intervention for individuals with mild to moderate anxiety and depression. Results revealed the self-help ACT intervention increased psychological flexibility and decreased anxiety. Additionally, at the three-month follow-up the results were maintained. Therefore, ACT self-help models, such as those reviewed in this guidebook, show promising results in helping anxious teens.

Psychological flexibility is "the ability to contact the present moment more fully as a conscious human being, and to change or persist in behavior when doing so serves valued ends" (Swain *et al.* 2013, p.966). Often, people who are not psychologically flexible struggle with maladaptive and unwanted thoughts and experiences. Psychological flexibility teaches clients to:

- live in the moment

- not try to control everything

- accept things for what they are (a negative thought or experience).

This shift in perspective can improve overall quality of life and assist clients in living a life that is in line with their personal values.

Swain *et al.* (2013) conducted a systematic literary review of ACT and anxiety to illustrate its effectiveness. ACT emphasizes the use of psychological flexibility to cope with unwanted negative experiences. ACT is a hexaflex model that is centered on six core processes:

1. cognitive defusion: learning methods to "step back" and recognize thoughts as being separate from the events they are associated with

2. acceptance: allowing thoughts to come and go without a struggle and recognizing them for what they are: "just thoughts"

3. living in the present moment: being fully aware of the "here and now," and learning to engage fully in what's happening right now

4. observing the self: being able to step outside oneself and to see the "whole self" i.e. physical self, thoughts, and emotions

5. values: discovering what is most important in one's life

6. committed action: living a value-driven life. Setting goals guided by life values and committing to live life according to those values.

(Hayes, Strosahl and Wilson 2012)

According to Codd *et al.* (2011) anxiety lessens in response to ACT, with gains continuing to be made even at the time of follow-up. In fact, their study found that some of the participants were symptom free and no longer met the diagnostic criteria of an anxiety disorder. In regards to panic disorders, ACT has individuals mindfully focus on values-based action and notice panic experiences as events that come and go. This is different from traditional CBT which aims to control and challenge faulty and distorted thinking patterns. ACT's aim is not to reduce the individual's emotional arousal, but to practice acceptance of his/her private inner experiences and enhance the ability to be more flexible (Luoma, Hayes, and Walser 2007).

In summary, utilizing an ACT protocol which incorporates acceptance, defusion, and values-based actions with the combination of exposure therapy is an effective treatment protocol for individuals suffering from an anxiety disorder (Meuret *et al.* 2012).While ACT has not been around as long as CBT, it is yielding very promising results for the future.

Unifying CBT and ACT

Does there have to be just one treatment approach? If research is showing strong results in favor of two treatment protocols, why not use both (Craske *et al.* 2012)? The two are not really all that different. Both ACT and CBT fall under the umbrella of behavioral psychology. Although the focus may vary at times from focusing on thoughts to accepting thoughts, the premise is the same, to help clients live a more meaningful and fulfilling life.

Arch *et al.* (2012) compared ACT and CBT in a mixed anxiety sample. They found that both ACT and CBT are effective in the treatment of anxiety disorders. When Arch and Craske (2008) examined the similarities and differences between CBT and ACT for the treatment of anxiety they concluded that the two approaches have as many similarities as differences. CBT and ACT share a common vision and purpose to reduce client pain and suffering.

Some would say that CBT tries to help clients reframe their thoughts and challenge their irrational beliefs. In opposition, ACT does not try to change thoughts and beliefs but teaches clients to accept the thoughts and try to defuse their emotional charge. However, some would argue that there are some self-destructive thoughts that need to be disputed and reframed and there are also things that we need to learn to accept and not fight.

So by integrating the two approaches you could focus on changing the things you want to change, exercising a certain degree of restraint, and accepting others that you cannot change. You could also learn not to re-play hurtful thoughts over and over again or to beat yourself up over a thought. One of the best things that comes out of ACT is staying in the "here and now" and being mindful of what is happening around you.

So, in conclusion, the gap between CBT and ACT is relatively small and can be bridged by creating an efficient and effective means to treat anxious clients (Ciarrochi and Bailey 2008). With treatment approaches now in place, it's time to move to one of the most important components of therapy…*you.*

Your role—the therapist

The role of the therapist is fundamental in the treatment of anxiety. The therapist can have a significant impact on therapeutic gains in counseling. Research indicates that therapists' style, integrity, and anxiety experience are indeed significant factors affecting therapeutic outcomes (e.g. Podell *et al.* 2013). Therapists who are perceived by clients as supportive yield more favorable therapeutic outcomes (Kendall *et al.* 2012). Additionally, the therapist's behavior, relationship with the client, and client involvement support change in therapy. If the client likes the therapist and feels a connection with him/her, the client experiences more treatment gains than one who does not connect in therapy. A positive collaboration between the two parties has been identified as a significant predictor to favorable client gains (Kendall *et al.* 2012; Podell *et al.* 2013). In order for you to best do your job it's important to know what anxiety condition your client is facing.

Anxiety diagnosis

"Anxiety disorder" is a general term which includes several different forms of abnormal, pathological anxieties, fears, and phobias. Clinically, it is a psychological and physiological state characterized by cognitive, somatic, emotional, and behavioral components. These components combine to create an unpleasant feeling that is typically associated with uneasiness, fear, and excessive worry. While each anxiety disorder has different symptoms, all the symptoms tend to cluster around excessive, irrational fear and dread.

With the release of the DSM-5 (American Psychiatric Association 2013), anxiety disorders remained relatively the same as in previous iterations, with only a few minor changes. Some of these changes include a reorganization of Obsessive Compulsive Disorder (OCD) from the classification of Anxiety Disorder to its own distinct category: Obsessive-Compulsive and Related Disorders. This removal was based on the emergence of evidence indicating that OCD is not only directly associated with anxiety, but also with other disorders, that is tics, somatoforms, grooming, and mood disorders. Similarly, Post Traumatic Stress Disorder and Acute Stress Disorder were independently classified as a distinct category: Trauma- and Stressor-Related Disorders. In addition, the specifier "anxious distressed" was added to the Depressive Disorders and Bipolar and Related Disorders categories in the DSM-5. Anxiety has been noted to be a significant feature of bipolar and major depressive disorder (Reichenberg 2014).

The following is a condensed reference highlighting each anxiety diagnosis, covered in this book. Due to the high co-morbidity of anxiety with Obsessive-Compulsive Disorders and Trauma- and Stressor-Related Disorders, some of the criteria that were previously deemed an Anxiety Disorder in the DSM-IV-TR (American Psychiatric Association 2000) are covered in this manual as well. This section will explore the various types of anxiety disorders and other related disorders in the DSM-5 and International Classification of Diseases (ICD)-10 (World Health Organization 2010).

Anxiety disorders
Separation Anxiety Disorder
Diagnostic/essential features
Extreme fear and/or anxiety focused on separation from home or attachment figures.

Characteristics

- Excessive worry or fear of being lost and unable to return to home or family.

- Fear of something bad happening to a major attachment figure during, or because of, the separation.Persistent reluctance or refusal to go to school or anywhere else due to fear of separation.

- Excessive fear of or reluctance towards being alone or without major attachment figures at home or in other settings.

- Repeated nightmares centered on being separated from a major attachment figure.

Selective Mutism

Diagnostic/essential features

Lack of speech when in social interactions with others.

Characteristics

- Failure to speak in social situations.

- Disturbance interferes with school, work, or with social communication.

Specific Phobia

Diagnostic/essential features

Irrational fear and anxiety caused by an object or situation

Characteristics

- Irrational fear of something e.g. heights or spiders.

- Facing the fear inducing stimulus results in extreme anxiety and possibly panic attacks.

- The anxiety producing stimulus is avoided if possible.

- The level of anxiety is markedly out of proportion to the danger the stimulus can cause.

Social Anxiety Disorder (Formerly the DSM-IV-TR diagnosis for Social Phobia)

Diagnostic/essential features

Intense, excessive fear and/or anxiety of social situations in which the individual fears being judged by others.

Characteristics

- Marked fear or anxiety centered on social situations.

- Fear of embarrassment or judgment.

- Social situations may cause extreme anxiety and possibly panic attacks.

- Anticipation of social events provokes fear and severe anxiety.

- Avoidance of social situations interferes with the quality of life.

Panic Disorder
Diagnostic/essential features
Recurrent unexpected panic attacks. Panic attacks marked by periods of intense fear.

Characteristics

- Regular panic attacks (rapid heartbeat, chest pain, shortness of breath, dizziness, and feelings of dying or losing control).

- Fear or excessive worry of experiencing another panic attack.

- Panic attacks significantly interfere with the quality of life.

- Panic attacks alter the individual's behavior.

Agoraphobia
Diagnostic/essential features
Excessive worry or anxiety activated by different situations and/or events.

Characteristics

- Fear of leaving home, unfamiliar places, or places that may be hard to escape.

- Frequently occurs as a result of panic attacks.

- Active avoidance of agoraphobic situations.

- Significantly affects the quality of life.

Other related disorders
Generalized Anxiety Disorder
Diagnostic/essential features
Anxiety and worry that is out of proportion to reality.

Characteristics

- Excessive anxiety and worry occur more often than not.

- Individuals experience difficulty controlling the anxiety or worry.

- Symptoms include but are not limited to restlessness, fatigue, irritability, difficulty concentrating, and problems sleeping.

- Symptoms cause significant life impairments.

Obsessive Compulsive Disorder

Diagnostic/essential features

Presence of obsessions and compulsions. Obsessions are repetitive or persistent thoughts, or impulses that reoccur. Compulsions are a response to an obsession. They are repetitve behaviours that an individual feels compelled to perform.

Characteristics

- Recurrent or persistent thoughts, images, and urges that are experienced and cause marked distress.

- Individual tries to suppress unwanted thoughts or behaviors, but to no avail.

- Obsessive thoughts may be about everyday life and may be aggressive and violent, sexual, or taboo in nature.

- Behaviors are used to try to stop or reduce the anxiety-provoking and unwanted thoughts.

Post Traumatic Stress Disorder

Diagnostic/essential features

Psychological distress and symptoms following exposure to a terrifying or traumatic event.

Characteristics

- Marked anxiety following experiencing, witnessing, or being exposed to a traumatic event.

- Individual may relive the event over and over again, either through flashbacks, memories, or emotions.

- Difficulty confronting the traumatic event—may alter behaviors to avoid reminders of the event.

Disclaimer

When making any clinical diagnosis, please consult the *Diagnostic and Statistical Manual* for appropriate categorization to make a proper diagnosis. This section is not to be used as a diagnostic manual, but rather as a resource to help you better understand adolescents who have either been diagnosed with an anxiety disorder or suffer from anxiety symptoms. Please refer to the DSM-5 or ICD-10 when making any clinical diagnosis.

Goal setting

Goal setting is an important tool in therapy. It serves as a compass leading to the values and things that clients hold dear. A common goal most clients will want to set is to eliminate anxiety. This is not a beneficial goal because anxiety is still going to exist in life, so the goal is unobtainable. Clients want to rid themselves completely of anxiety and may be resistant to confronting situations that cause them discomfort or anxiety. As a result they may stop going to therapy and feel that it is a failure because they still feel anxious. So, rather than letting clients feel that therapy will entirely eliminate anxiety, it's best to have them work through anxiety with success. They can also become active observers of their thoughts and behaviors and learn coping mechanisms to overcome their anxiety.

Using *Teen Anxiety* in group therapy

You can use *Teen Anxiety* in a group format. It can be laid out in nine weekly small group sessions incorporating didactic elements, mindfulness exercises, experiential exercises, group discussion/processes, and homework (activities from *Teen Anxiety*). Themes surrounding psychological flexibility in relation to values-driven committed action will be interwoven into the sessions. Group facilitators are encouraged to integrate the interpersonal group process into the curriculum and openly engage members in the exploration of acceptance, mindfulness, and values.

Treatment

The group content is designed to include common CBT and ACT elements and anxiety disorder-specific treatment elements. Teen clients should make a commitment to engage in assigned homework tasks, all of which should be recorded on a homework log (template found in Part III) and discussed in each session.

Each group meeting is organized roughly as follows:

- Review of homework from the previous week.

- Didactic segment (themes from each chapter of *Teen Anxiety*) with group discussion.

- Experiential exercise with group discussion—each chapter has an activity that you can use to meet this purpose.

- Close with a mindfulness activity—each chapter includes a mindfulness activity.

- Group discussion/process.

- Assigning *Teen Anxiety* exercises for next week's session.

Remind participants to record information on their homework log

The order of group sessions is as follows:

- Session 1: Introductions/goal setting.

- Session 2: Understanding how anxiety is affecting your life.

  ○ Experiential Activity: 1.9

  ○ Mindfulness Activity: 1.6

  ○ Experiential Activity: 2.1; 2.3

  ○ Mindfulness Activity: 2.8

- Session 3: Exploring the mind and body interaction.
  - Experiential Activity: 2.1; 2.3
  - Mindfulness Activity: 2.8

- Session 4: Distancing yourself from and letting go of unhelpful thoughts and beliefs.
  - Experiential Activity: 3.1; 3.5
  - Mindfulness Activity: 3.8

- Session 5: Letting go of the baggage/Being aware and in tune with your emotions.
  - Experiential Activity: 4.1; 4.2
  - Mindfulness Activity: 4.8

- Session 6: Perfectly imperfect/Understanding how your thoughts and feelings drive your actions.
  - Experiential Activity: 5.2; 5.3
  - Mindfulness Activity: 5.9

- Session 7: Coping and observing self/Being aware of what you are thinking, feeling and doing.
  - Experiential Activity: 6.1; 6.5; 6.6
  - Mindfulness Activity: 6.8

- Session 8: The power of letting go/Living a life of values, goals and actions.
  - Experiential Activity: 7.2; 7.8
  - Mindfulness Activity: 7.3

- Session 9: Conclusion and tie in with all group themes. Put emphasis on committed action in alliance with values.
  - Experiential Activity: 7.9; 7.10
  - Mindfulness Activity: 7.4

Conclusion to Part I

What is the future of treating teen anxiety? According to Kendall *et al.* (2012) we have no worries, because new approaches are showing promising results. Anxiety affects about 20 percent of the population, with the majority of onsets occurring during the childhood and adolescent years (Low *et al.* 2012; Swain *et al.* 2013). If left undetected or untreated, anxiety can unveil itself in adulthood causing other mental issues such as depression, substance abuse and significant interference with relationships and daily functioning. Anxiety in young people can be treated, but not all teens reap positive outcomes. There are advantageous treatment options for these anxious youths.

With approximately 60–65 percent of youths responding to CBT, it is not a surprise that it is considered the most favored approach. However, research indicates that about a third of anxious youths do not respond to traditional CBT (Kerns *et al.* 2013). What keeps some from responding and some from not responding to treatment? That is the question that many counselors are still trying to answer in the quest to find the best treatment approach for anxious youths.

Other important components to treating anxiety include understanding the executive functioning and brain development of the adolescent. Adolescents are in a state of transition and change, not only psychologically, but also physiologically. It is paramount for therapists to take the whole picture into account in designing a treatment plan. The developing prefrontal cortex may help to explain the impulsive, irrational thinking skills, and risk-taking behaviors that often accompany the adolescent years.

The role of executive functioning can assist in the development of higher order thinking. Research supports the idea that executive functioning can be strengthened by the use of social skills training, working through moral dilemmas and practicing higher level decision-making skills (Casey *et al.* 2011; Pharo *et al.* 2011).

Aside from brain development, parenting styles have shown a strong correlation with teen anxiety. Research has found that parents of anxious children tend to be anxious, demanding, controlling, less affectionate, and overprotective (Kendall *et al.* 2012). Understanding parenting styles is essential in designing a treatment plan not only to address the individual, but also to incorporate parents into therapy sessions.

Another key component to helping clients work through anxiety is the therapeutic relationship. Aspects such as therapist behavior, rapport, relationship with the client, and support promote positive therapeutic gains (Podell *et al.* 2013). If the youth likes the therapist and feels a connection with him/her, the young person will get more out of therapy than one who does not connect in therapy. A positive collaboration between the two parties has been identified as a significant predictor to therapeutic gains. Additionally, counselor training and competency are important. Counselors need to be competent and up to date with the literature available on the treatment of anxiety (Podell *et al.* 2013).

On a final note, unfortunately there are still barriers to receiving adequate treatment. From mental health stigmatization to finances, transportation, and scheduling, there are many obstacles that may keep a child from receiving appropriate care. However, there is an increase in accessibility treatments and many different avenues are being utilized to reach these youths.

In summary, anxiety disorders are predecessors to adult mental health disorders. Effective treatment in childhood pays off well in adulthood. With the use of empirically supported approaches such as CBT and ACT and other innovative approaches, the future is looking bright for the treatment of teen anxiety.

LETTER TO A TEEN

Dear Reader

Odds are, if you're reading this right now then either you or someone who cares about you feels that you are struggling with anxiety. Anxiety is a normal emotion and we all experience it at some point in life. Teens, such as you, are particularly susceptible to anxiety because of all the physical, emotional, and psychological changes they're going through. You're growing up and to add to it, you're faced with many dilemmas and decisions. Some of these decisions have the potential of being life altering. The older you get the more responsibility gets shifted your way, and while that may seem great at times it can also be tough. From school to friendships you have many things to sort through. Life is complex, and trying to make sense of it is no easy task.

While anxiety may feel overwhelming and unbearable at times, there is good news; it is totally treatable. You are not alone and you can overcome your anxiety. Lots of teens have trouble with anxiety. Did you know that you can learn to channel and control your anxious feelings? It's true, just like you learned how to wait your turn in line, share with other children, ride your bike, and even tie your shoelaces, you can learn how to control the feeling of anxiety.

In fact, you have already taken the first step to getting help by working with your counselor through this book. By working through the activities in this book you are taking an important step toward empowering yourself and not being a victim of anxiety any longer. *Teen Anxiety* will teach you all the important skills to help you divide, conquer, and accept your anxiety.

Here are a few things you will learn:

- what triggers your anxiety

- the importance of taking care of yourself

- how to work through anxious feelings, fear, stress, and panic

- most importantly, how to accept and manage your thoughts and emotions.

While all of these skills are necessary in helping you overcome anxiety, there may be times when you have to explore some uncomfortable feelings, but once you conquer them you will feel better. In order to gain the full benefit of *Teen Anxiety*, it is important that you follow the activities that your therapist prescribes for you. Also, you should spend time practicing the skills you learn over and over again. As with most things in life, the more time and practice you put into working on your anxiety, the more you'll get out of it. By completing this treatment program, you will feel more empowered, more confident, and more secure in who you are. Are you ready to start the journey to become anxiety free?

Empowering you with confidence and success,

Raychelle Cassada Lohmann

Part II

ACTIVITIES

Chapter One

DEFINING AND UNDERSTANDING ANXIETY

Being anxious is a normal feeling. In fact, anxiety is a motivating force that compels us to take action. However, when it becomes persistent and overtakes seconds, minutes, and hours then it is no longer normal. Fortunately, there are steps we can take to reduce our symptoms and regain control and normalcy of our lives.

Chapter outline

Activity 1.1 Defining Anxiety

Activity 1.2 Anxiety Symptoms

Activity 1.3 Anxiety Triggers

Activity 1.4 Anxiety Patterns

Activity 1.5 Anxiety Profile

Activity 1.6 Emotional Acceptance

Activity 1.7 Stress Relief Journal

Activity 1.8 A Helping Hand

Activity 1.9 Values Compass

Chapter objectives

From this chapter you will:

- define and understand anxiety

- explore anxiety symptoms

- identify types of anxiety disorders

- explore maladaptive coping strategies and confront your client's agenda

- help your clients set up a self-monitoring system

- assist your client in setting goals and identifying values.

Pre-/post-scaling questions

Pre-question

This group of activities will help you better understand your anxiety and how it is affecting your life. On a scale of 0 to 10, with zero being "no understanding" and 10 being "full understanding," rate how much you understand how this thing called "anxiety" is affecting your life. Plot the score on the grid below.

Post-question

This group of activities reviewed anxiety and how it is affecting your life. At the beginning of this chapter you rated yourself at a _____ (let them know the pre-score rating). Using the same scale of 0 to 10, with zero being "no understanding" and 10 being "full understanding," rate where you are now in understanding how anxiety is affecting your life. Plot the post-score on the grid below.

Here are some sample follow-up questions that can assist you in comparing and contrasting your client's scores:

- "I noticed that you moved from a '2' to a '6' on the scale. What are some things that helped you move up?"

- "I noticed that you moved down or stayed the same on the scale. What are some things that can help you move up on the scale?"

- "What are some things that can help you move up on the scale?"

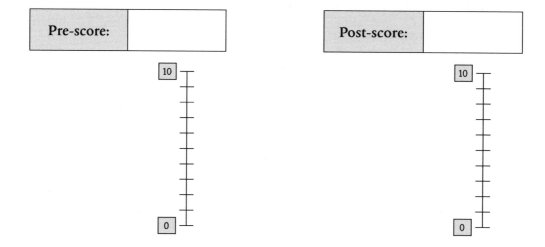

DEFINING ANXIETY

INTRODUCTION

Anxiety is defined as the feeling of apprehension, stress, and worry. While it is completely normal to feel anxious at times, it's not okay to carry around the burden of feeling anxious all of the time. When anxiety saturates the majority of your days, then it has gone beyond the scope of what is considered "normal." Look at Jordan's example. His anxiety reached the point that it not only consumed him internally, but it also affected him externally.

One night Jordan was in his room thinking about his girlfriend Rachel. This was Rachel's final year in school. Next year she'd be off to college. He couldn't imagine his life without her. He still had one more year before he graduated... What would he do without her? The more Jordan thought about Rachel leaving the more anxious and nervous he became. In a matter of minutes, his thoughts of losing her overtook him. While at first his feelings were perfectly normal, they crossed the line when they became so intense they made him physically ill. His stomach started churning and gurgling while sweat started beading across his forehead. Before long he was hunched over the toilet heaving.

Jordan's mother heard him in the bathroom and went to check on him. She assumed something may have been bothering him because unfortunately he usually had stomach problems when something was bothering him. He had always been an anxious child... Plus, she noticed he had started biting his nails again. When she got to the bathroom, Jordan's arms were folded over his head on the rim of the toilet and he was heaving again. His mother consoled him by putting her arms around him. After some coaxing, she got Jordan to tell her what had made him so upset.

Jordan explained that Rachel had just got accepted into her number one choice of colleges, and it was over six hours away from home...and from him. "Jordan, this has been going on for a while. I think this may be more than a fear of losing Rachel. For some time now I have suspected that you have a problem with anxiety, but I didn't know it was this bad. I think it's time that we got you some help... You don't have to go through this anymore... With the right tools you can overcome worry instead of making yourself sick all the time." Jordan's mom helped him feel better and she used a word that struck a chord. He now had a word for this powerful feeling he struggled with—"anxiety."

DIRECTIONS

Can you relate to Jordan's story? Have you struggled with anxiety to the point that it made you physically sick? If so, you are not alone. It is estimated that anxiety affects one in five people and many of those people don't seek help. What makes you different is that you do want to change, and you do want help. To begin with it is important to identify what anxiety does to you. Read the feeling words and circle the ones you've experienced in association with anxiety.

Afraid	Distressed	Indecisive	Remorseful
Agitated	Distracted	Indifferent	Removed
Alarmed	Distraught	Insecure	Resentful
Alienated	Enraged	Instable	Reserved
Aloof	Exhausted	Irate	Restless
Angry	Embarrassed	Irritable	Scared
Annoyed	Fidgety	Irritated	Self-conscious
Anxious	Flustered	Isolated	Stressed out
Apprehensive	Forgetful	Lethargic	Suspicious
Ashamed	Fragile	Lonely	Tense
Bewildered	Frightened	Lost	Terrified
Bored	Frustrated	Miserable	Tired
Confused	Gloomy	Mistrustful	Troubled
Cranky	Guarded	Moody	Turbulent
Depleted	Guilty	Nervous	Uncomfortable
Depressed	Hesitant	Overwhelmed	Uneasy
Despairing	Helpless	Panicked	Unhappy
Detached	Hopeless	Petrified	Uninterested
Devastated	Horrified	Puzzled	Unsettled
Disappointed	Hostile	Rattled	Withdrawn
Discouraged	Hurt	Reckless	Worried
Disheartened	Impulsive	Regretful	Withdrawn

1. How many words did you circle?

2. Were there any other words that you feel that were not on the list? If so, write them down.

3. Rank in order the top five feelings that you've experienced the most.

EXPAND ON IT

Answer the following questions:

1. Of the feelings that you identified, list the one that bothers you the most.

2. How often do you experience the feeling that you identified? For example three or four times a day, or two or three times a week?

3. When was the last time you experienced this feeling?

4. Describe what was going on when you were feeling it.

5. List the things that you do to try to stop feeling it. Do they work? Explain.

6. What things do you do that help you to alleviate your anxiety?

Activity 1.2

ANXIETY SYMPTOMS

INTRODUCTION

There are many symptoms that point to anxiety; some people experience a few, while others experience many. Some symptoms may come and go while others linger. It is important to understand what your symptoms are and how much they keep you from enjoying your daily life.

Meredith had a huge presentation due in her literature class. As a part of the assignment, she had to do a skit about a story that the class had read. For most students this was no problem, but to Meredith it was nerve-wracking. Her number one fear was speaking in front of other people. She kept asking herself, "What are they going to think of me? I'm a loser? A screw-up?" Meredith sat back and watched all of the other skits. They were great, some were witty, some were serious, and some were just goofy, but fun. Everyone did a great job. It seemed so easy for them. Meredith wished she was like that, but instead she was thinking, "I'm going to die up there. How am I supposed to stand in front of the whole class by myself?" Meredith's heart was beating so loud she barely heard the teacher say, "Meredith, you're up."

The very thought of the skit made Meredith's heart race. She just knew she'd make a fool of herself in front of everybody. "I'm trapped, screw-up, screw-up, there's no way out of this screw-up." Meredith felt her fear seize her body and she became paralyzed. Meredith looked at the door and bolted. "I've got to get a grip, I can't keep on living my life like this." She bent down and sat leaning her back against the lockers. Mr. Riddle, the assistant principal, walked by and saw Meredith sitting in the hall. He bent down and started to talk to her. "Come with me," he said. Meredith slowly got up and walked with him to his office. He told her to have a seat and started talking to her about what had happened. He got up and went to his bookshelf. He pulled a book off of the shelf and opened it. "Here, check off as many of these that fit," he said.

Meredith looked at the page. The header said "Anxiety Checklist." She was supposed to check off all of her symptoms and then work through the rest of the book and learn what to do when she became anxious. After completing the activity, Meredith realized it wasn't just fear she was battling, she had a problem with anxiety. Mr. Riddle saw that she had a lot of symptoms checked, so he said, "Meredith, I want you to borrow this book from me and work on it." She decided that she would work through the book a little at a time. As she was getting ready to close the cover, something jumped off the page and spoke to her. Inside the cover in bold and italicized print were the words "Anxiety is treatable." For some reason those words resonated with her and she closed the book feeling a sense of hope for the first time in a long time. With a smile on her face, she said, "Thanks, Mr. Riddle...I think this is just what I need."

DIRECTIONS

Below is an anxiety symptom checklist. Look over the symptoms and mark the ones that you have experienced.

Anxiety symptom checklist

- ❑ Feelings of panic
- ❑ Feelings of fear
- ❑ Uneasiness
- ❑ Uncontrollable thoughts
- ❑ Repeated thoughts of traumatic experiences
- ❑ Nightmares
- ❑ Compulsive behaviors (such as constantly checking to make sure you have switched an appliance off or locked the door)
- ❑ Problems sleeping
- ❑ Sweaty hands and/or feet
- ❑ Difficulty breathing
- ❑ Racing heartbeats
- ❑ An inability to be still and calm/constantly fidgeting
- ❑ Nausea
- ❑ Muscle tension
- ❑ Dizziness/lightheadedness
- ❑ Chest pain
- ❑ Stomach problems
- ❑ Irritability
- ❑ Headaches
- ❑ Grinding teeth
- ❑ Trouble concentrating
- ❑ Weight loss/gain
- ❑ Moodiness
- ❑ Increase in risk-taking behavior (smoking, drinking, engaging in promiscuous behavior)
- ❑ Fatigue
- ❑ Trembling
- ❑ Self-injury

★

☐ Nail biting

☐ Frequent crying

☐ Body aches

☐ Explosive anger

☐ Avoiding anxiety-producing situations

☐ Social withdrawal

☐ Feeling of failure

☐ Constantly worrying about something for no reason

☐ Continually obsessing about doing something wrong

☐ Extreme panic which leads to the inability to perform or function in certain situations.

EXPAND ON IT ←—→

Now that you have identified your anxious symptoms, follow up by answering the following questions:

1. Describe any other symptom, not listed, that you have experienced.

2. Which of the circled symptoms cause you a little discomfort?

3. Which of the circled symptoms cause you a lot of discomfort?

4. Beside each symptom listed, write how long you have experienced it.

5. Rewrite the following statement on a separate piece of paper and put it in an area where you can see it. "Anxiety is treatable. I can overcome this."

Anxiety can be a serious condition. If it is impairing your day-to-day life, please get help, especially if you've been feeling this way for months. Share what you are experiencing with a therapist, parent, teacher, or another trusted adult.

ANXIETY TRIGGERS

INTRODUCTION

We all have things in our lives that cause us to be stressed and anxious. Imagine your life as a large control panel with a lot of buttons. Each button represents things that make you feel anxious, embarrassed, stressed, ashamed, insecure, panicky, and nervous. When the button is pushed you get all worked up and become anxious. Those buttons are called your anxiety triggers, because when pushed they trigger an anxious response.

Some common anxiety triggers are:

- getting up and speaking in front of others

- being made fun of

- walking into crowded rooms

- eating in front of other people

- driving

- getting hurt

- water, spiders, rats, or some other creature that scares you.

It's important to know what your anxiety triggers are so you can be prepared and ready to handle situations that press your buttons.

DIRECTIONS

The circles on the next page represent buttons on your own control panel of life. List as many things that trigger your anxiety that you can think of in the first row of buttons. Color these buttons red. List as many things that reduce your anxiety that you can think of. Color these buttons green.

Anxiety triggers
(list things that make you anxious)

Anxiety reducers
(list things that help you calm down)

Getting called on
in front of other people.

Doodling and drawing.

EXPAND ON IT

Answer the following questions:

1. When was the last time one of your triggers was activated? Describe what happened and how you felt in the space below.

2. How often do your triggers get activated? Circle the appropriate answer:

   Daily   How many times a day?

   Weekly   How many times a week?

3. List the things you do to help you feel better when you're stressed or anxious.

4. Write how often you do things that you enjoy. Circle the appropriate answer:

   Daily   How many times a day?

   Weekly   How many times a week?

Make a plan to do one activity you enjoy doing tomorrow. Write down the activity that you chose.

Activity 1.4

ANXIETY PATTERNS

INTRODUCTION

Research has shown time and time again that people who write down and monitor their behavior have greater success in changing it than those who don't. By monitoring your anxiety you increase your awareness to it. You'll be amazed at how keeping track of your anxiety will help you recognize:

- the types of situations that cause stress or anxiety

- when you are more susceptible to anxiety—for example, do you become more anxious when you're tired?

- people who provoke your anxiety

- patterns in your anxiety response

- how you behave when you're anxious.

Changing your response to anxiety will involve making a lifestyle change, but by taking the right steps you can divide and conquer your anxiety.

DIRECTIONS

During the next two weeks use the *Anxiety log* to get a snapshot of your anxiety. This will help you discover *when, where,* and *how* your anxiety is affecting you. Pay special attention to *when you become anxious, where it's happening, how you feel,* and *what you are thinking.* When you feel anxious or stressed, write down what's happening as soon as you can. That way you'll get a good picture of what's happening during an anxious episode.

Anxiety log

Time	Date	Location	Situation	Feelings	Thoughts

★

Next, rate each anxious episode on your anxiety log. Use the following rating scale for anxiety intensity:

Somewhat anxious = 1 (for example, you may feel jittery or as if you have knots in your stomach)

Moderately anxious = 2 (for example, you may try to make excuses to get out of the situation or you may start biting your nails)

Very anxious = 3 (for example, you avoid situations at all cost or you get physically sick, nauseous, or have severe headaches. You may even experience a full-blown panic attack)

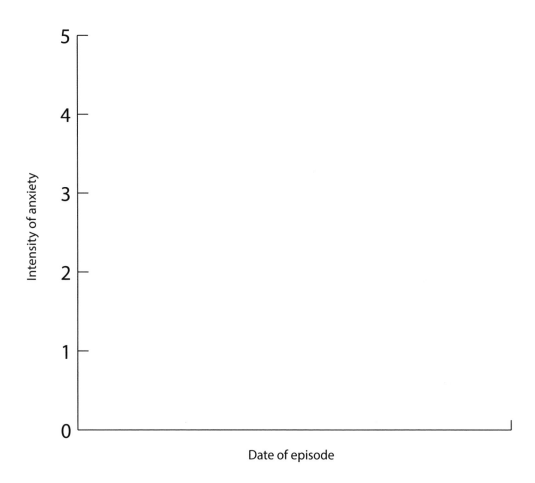

EXPAND ON IT

Use your anxiety log to answer the following questions:

1. Describe any patterns you noticed in your anxiety. For example, did you get more anxious when you were at school or before going to school? Perhaps you were more anxious in the morning before beginning your day or at night before bed when everything from the day was playing over and over again in your head.

2. List the things that triggered your anxiety. Were there things that you could have done to prevent yourself from getting so worked up?

3. Overall, how do you feel you handled your anxiety? List the areas that you need to improve on the most.

4. Did you notice when your anxiety escalated? Were there any warning signs that told you that anxiety and stress were coming on? If so, list them.

5. Describe how keeping track of your anxiety can help you control it.

Activity 1.5

ANXIETY PROFILE

INTRODUCTION

Creating an anxiety profile is a great way to help you explore how anxiety is affecting you. Sometimes it's hard to put feelings into words, but when you put them down on paper you can see what you need to work on. A profile can help you do just that.

Taylor laid her head on her desk at school. She was exhausted; she hadn't been sleeping well and the dark circles under her eyes were becoming hard to mask with concealer. Not only was she exhausted but her grades were suffering too. It was too much for Taylor to deal with, so she did what she normally did when she became overwhelmed...she laid her head down on the desk and dozed off. She was so sound asleep that she didn't even hear the bell ring.

Ms. Henry went up to Taylor's desk and gently shook her shoulder. Taylor lifted her head and realized where she was. Startled, she jumped up and started collecting her things. "Taylor, this isn't like you. What's going on? Your grades have slipped and now you're sleeping in class?" Taylor confided in Ms. Henry, about how she couldn't focus anymore and she couldn't sleep because she lay in bed at night worried about school, home, and work. "I just can't seem to get it together, Ms. Henry," she said. "I worry all the time about everything. I never used to be like this... I don't like how I feel. It's so hard to come to school..."

Ms. Henry listened to Taylor and added, "That sounds like anxiety. I too once battled it, so I understand how it can make you feel. Let's map out what's going on by creating a profile that takes you through anxiety characteristics. Then I think we need to go and see the school counselor and take it from there. Taylor," Ms. Henry said with a smile and a wink, "notice how I said 'I too once battled anxiety?' I used the past tense for a reason. With the right treatment your anxiety can be a thing of the past too." Taylor felt relieved to have someone who finally understood what she was going through. Ms. Henry sat with Taylor as she created an anxiety profile to help her understand how anxiety was affecting her.

DIRECTIONS

Like Taylor, create your own anxiety profile. Begin by reading each statement and answer "yes" or "no."

1. I constantly worry about something.

2. If I don't have anything to worry about, I find something.

3. I have trouble sleeping.

4. I eat more or less than I used to.

5. Anxiety affects my body.

6. I often panic.

7. I feel that people don't understand me.

8. Others have commented that I worry too much.

9. I often feel alone.

10. I keep playing out "what ifs" over and over in my head.

11. I worry about what others think of me.

12. I am afraid of being a failure.

13. I obsess over things.

14. My anxiety keeps me from accomplishing things in life.

15. I spend most of my time worrying about things that never happen.

For each of the statements below circle the number that best describes you.

16. How often do you spend worrying about why you do the things that you do?

Please circle only one answer.

1	2	3	4	5
All the time	Often	Sometimes	Rarely	None of the time

17. How do you usually respond to anxiety?

Please circle all that apply.

1	2	3	4	5
Run away from the situation	Cry	Shut down	Act out in anger	Freeze up

Other:

18. On average how often do you feel anxious?

Please circle only one answer.

1	2	3	4
More than once a day	Once a day	More than once per week	Once per week

19. If you answered "yes" to question 16, how much time are you willing to devote to working on the activities in this workbook?

Please circle only one answer.

1	2	3	4
Once a day	A few times a week	Once per week	Whenever you have time

20. Identify the area of your life that causes you the most stress:

1	2	3	4	5
Parents	Boyfriend/ Girlfriend	School	Friends	Siblings

List any other area:

Understanding your profile results

The more frequently you answered "yes," to questions 1—15 and the higher you rated your responses, the more anxiety is affecting your life. By committing to the activities in this book, you will learn skills to help you gain control and overcome anxiety.

EXPAND ON IT

Your anxiety can be a thing of the past too. With time and patience you can conquer it. Sometimes it is good to think of what you wish would happen and then work on making it come true. Pretend that you have a magic wand and complete the following statements:

- I wish my anxiety would...

- I wish I could change...

- I wish I was able to...

- I wish therapy would help me with...

Activity 1.6

EMOTIONAL ACCEPTANCE

INTRODUCTION

Have you ever watched a wave in the ocean crash on the shore only to roll back into the ocean? The waves come and go. Some waves are more intense than others...some roll up lightly on the shore, while others hit with a hard impact. Regardless, of whether they are strong or weak, one thing remains the same...they all roll back into the ocean. Emotions and feelings are a lot like waves. Problems occur when we don't let them come and go, rather we hold onto them, torture ourselves with unwanted thoughts, and fight our inner experiences. This internal struggle only makes things worse and sometimes makes the anxiety stick around. That's why it is important to let thoughts come and go like waves in an ocean and recognize them for what they are...an emotion, a feeling, a thought...nothing more, nothing less. This process is called *acceptance*.

DIRECTIONS

To illustrate how much more difficult it is to fight something try this activity.

You'll need:

- a timing device
- paper
- a writing utensil
- a banana—if you don't have one, draw one on a piece of paper.

Look at the banana, say the word a few times, smell it. Now set it aside. Next, set your timer to 60 seconds.

Your assignment

Do not think of a banana for the next 60 seconds. Don't think of how it looks, smells, tastes, the color, the shape, etc. Fight the thought of the banana with all your might. If you catch yourself thinking of a banana, place a tally mark on the paper.

After 60 seconds: okay, fess up. How many times did you think of a banana?

This activity wasn't as easy as it was set up to be. In fact, when you are told not to do something or to stop thinking or feeling a certain way it becomes even more difficult. But isn't that what you're doing when you're anxious? You're fighting thoughts and it isn't working. When you try not to think of something you think about it even more. In fact, it can consume you. One of the key points in these activities is that you don't have to fight your thoughts; you can accept them for what they are—thoughts... And just like a wave returns to the ocean, your anxious thought will also dissolve back into your mind.

Try this

For the next 60 seconds think about anything you want; if you think of a banana that's okay. If a banana crosses your mind let the thought freely come and go. Don't fight it like before.

Do you see a difference? Which exercise was easier, fighting or accepting the thought of a banana? You can apply this to anxious thoughts. If you are experiencing anxiety, don't fight it. Let it freely come and go. Fighting it will only make it worse.

EXPAND ON IT

Answer the following questions:

1. Describe a time when you fought your thoughts and feelings.

2. List reasons why fighting your thoughts and feelings can be harmful.

3. Describe how accepting your thoughts and feelings can help you feel better.

Activity 1.7

STRESS RELIEF JOURNAL

INTRODUCTION

Keeping a journal is a great way to cope with anxiety. Writing is a therapeutic tool to help you deal with life stressors, relieve stress, and reduce the amount of worrying. It is a great way for you to explore and cope with your problems rather than holding them in and letting them escalate.

The great thing about journaling is that you have no one to impress, so you can be honest and write freely about what you want to change.

Did you know that journaling can:

- let you sort out your thoughts and feelings

- allow you to reflect on your life

- provide an outlet for expressing your raw emotions

- release negative self-defeating thoughts so that you can focus on the positive things that are surrounding you

- provide you with a record of how much you have changed and grown?

DIRECTIONS

Journaling is super easy. All you need is a computer or paper and a pen. Whatever method you use to write, make sure that it's secure and confidential; you probably don't want someone to know every secret and struggle that you have. So if you use an electronic means to write, take extra precaution to keep your information safe and secure. Next, find a quiet, comfortable, and secluded place where you won't be disturbed.

Unlike school work, the cool thing about journaling is that there are no rules. You can write about anything that you want; grammar, punctuation, and syntax don't matter. Your entry can be as long or as short as you want it to be. Here are a couple of suggested methods that you can use to write in your journaling, but you can use any method you'd like.

Free expression writing

Write about anything that comes to mind (for example, how your day went, things you're looking forward to, personal struggles, or anything else you like). If you become stuck in your thoughts, begin by writing about your daily experience—you can even sketch a picture if you want. Your journal belongs to you, so you create and abide by your own rules.

Positives and negatives

Take a piece of paper and draw a line down the center of the page. If you're using a computer create a table with a line separating the columns.

On the left side let your anxiety do the talking. List all of your feelings, fears, stressors, and worries.	On the right side write a response to what you wrote down on the left side. If you can't come up with positive things on your own, think of someone who cares for you deeply...what would he or she tell you about that anxious talk?

Putting your thoughts on paper can be extremely helpful in coping with stress and anxiety. The next time you fear a dreaded situation, jot your thoughts down and pour out your fears and frustrations. So what are you waiting for? Get a piece of paper or turn on the computer and get started.

EXPAND ON IT

Look back at a few of your journal entries and answer the following questions:

1. Make a plan for putting journaling into your schedule:

   a. What's your location? Where are you going to write?

   b. When's the best time for you to write? For example, in the morning, during the day, or in the evening?

   c. What's your preferred method of journaling? For example, paper and pen, in a journal book, on a computer, or using another electronic device?

2. Describe how it felt to pour out your thoughts and feelings.

3. List how stress relief journaling can help you better cope with anxiety.

Activity 1.8

A HELPING HAND

INTRODUCTION

It doesn't take a rocket scientist to figure out that making a life change is hard. Change is a process not an event. Any time you want to change it will take time, patience, perseverance, and a helping hand. That's why it's important to align yourself with caring people who have your best interests at heart. These people will serve as a support system. Support systems work because they provide:

- a sense of belonging—sharing things with people who care about you and only want you to succeed may help you feel accepted

- emotional security—as you start to target your anxiety you may become sensitive and increasingly aware of how you're feeling. It's important to surround yourself with people you trust so you have a sounding board for your feelings when they arise

- encouragement—since these people only want what's in your best interest, they're going to want to help you reach your goals. Their encouragement will play a vital role in your success.

Healthy and supportive relationships can help reduce stress and anxiety. You don't have to be strong all the time—you can actually lean on someone to help you get through your hard times.

DIRECTIONS

Begin developing your support system by thinking about the top five people in your life who are:

- trustworthy

- encouraging

- supportive

- caring.

In the space provided, trace a copy of your hand. On each finger write each of your social supports. In the palm of your hand write ways your social supports can help you better cope with anxiety. For example:

- talk to me when I'm having a panic attack

- help me sort through difficult decisions

- encourage me when I want to back out of something that is good for me.

★

EXPAND ON IT

Now that you have your social supports, you are going to need to rely on them during your quest to change. Let your supports know that you are working on overcoming your anxiety and may need their help along the way. Tell them why you have chosen them and the positive role they play in your life. If you have trouble speaking to people then you can script out what you are going to say first. For example:

> *"I am going to start working on getting a handle on my anxiety and I need your help. Will you help me?"*

Your social supports will play a very important role in your anxiety treatment plan. Sometimes when you're stressed it's hard to think clearly. So place the names of your supports and their phone numbers in places that are easy to get to. Remember you can't do this alone, so draw on your supports to help you get through this.

Activity 1.9

VALUES COMPASS

INTRODUCTION

Values are the things we deem important or find meaningful in life. We all have them. They are our beliefs, ideas, or priorities. They are different for everyone and they change over the course of time. They serve as our compass in life; they provide us with vision, clarity, and direction. Values are not goals. Goals can be achieved, but values are the cornerstone to our goals.

Here are a couple of scenarios to help you see the difference between goals and values.

Scenario one

Emma was constantly running late to school. It was beginning to interfere with her grades and she was having to serve detention after school—not fun. So Emma decided to set a goal for the following week of getting to class on time. Emma took pride in her grades and being a good student and her tardiness was interfering with her values and desire to be a good student and a hard worker.

Goal—get to school on time.

Value—be a good student.

Scenario two

Michael took pride in being healthy and he wanted to get into better shape, so he decided that he'd go for a run daily. Michael's goal was running everyday but his value was to take care of his body.

Goal—run daily.

Value—be healthy and in shape.

DIRECTIONS

What values are on your compass? One way to think of your values is to think of yourself in old age. Imagine a group of people in the room talking about you. Unbeknownst to them, you overhear everything that they are saying. What kind of person would you want them to say you are (e.g. caring, kind, respectful)? What kind of life would you want them to say you live (e.g. a life of integrity, a life of loyalty)? What personality traits or characteristics would you like for them to say that you have (perseverance, ambitious, responsible)? The ways in which you want others to see you represent what is important to you. They are your values. You are constantly living in service of your values. You are striving to be the person you want to be. Values are not material things; they are ambitions, dreams, things that are important to you... Values represent who you are.

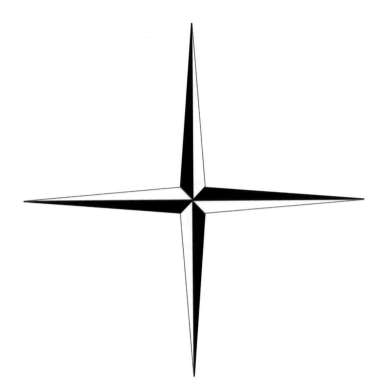

Let your values compass guide you as you navigate through your journey of freeing yourself from anxiety. You may want to copy your compass and put it in places that you can readily access (for example your dresser, bathroom mirror, on your phone (take a screenshot)). Your values compass will serve as a reminder of living your life based on what you deem is important.

EXPAND ON IT

Let your values guide you in life. For each value that you listed write some goals to help you live a value-driven life.

Value

Goal

Value

Goal

Value

Goal

Value

Goal

Chapter Two

ANXIETY AND THE BODY

Each time we experience a thought our body reacts. Negative, sad, worried, and anxious thoughts make us feel bad; but positive, happy, relaxed, and hope-filled thoughts make us feel good.

Chapter outline

Activity 2.1 Body Scan

Activity 2.2 Fight or Flight

Activity 2.3 The Power of a Breath

Activity 2.4 Healthy Eating

Activity 2.5 Exercise

Activity 2.6 A Good Night's Rest

Activity 2.7 Fit for Life

Activity 2.8 Mindfulness and the Body

Chapter objectives

From this chapter you will:

- learn body cues toward anxiety

- understand when the body's stress response system is activated

- learn proper breathing techniques

- understand how exercise can reduce anxiety and stress

- explore the benefits of getting adequate rest and healthy eating

- explore the benefits of avoiding foods that trigger anxiety

- learn mindfulness techniques to alleviate anxiety.

Pre-/post-scaling questions

Pre-question

On a scale of 0 to 10, with zero being "a little" and 10 being "a lot," rate your understanding of how anxiety affects your body. Plot the score on the grid below.

Post-question

We just finished covering all of the important things that you need to know about the interaction between your body and anxiety. Things that we take for granted such as what we eat, how much sleep we get, and even exercise can have an effect on how we feel. At the beginning of this chapter you rated yourself at a _____ (let them know the pre-score rating) for understanding your body and anxiety interaction. Using the same scale, of 0 to 10, with zero being "a little" and 10 being "a lot," rate where you are now in your understanding of the interaction between anxiety and your body. Plot the post-score on the grid below.

Here are some sample follow-up questions that can assist you in comparing and contrasting your client's scores:

"I noticed that you moved from a '3' to an '8' on the scale. What are some things that contributed to you moving up?"

"I noticed that you moved down or stayed the same on the scale. What are some things that can help you move up on the scale?"

"What are some things that you can do to help you move closer to a '10'?"

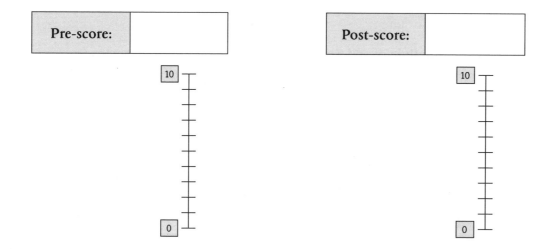

Activity 2.1

BODY SCAN

INTRODUCTION

A sweat broke out across Jared's brow. His fists were tightly clenched and his jaw ached from the tension. He struggled to get a full breath and for a moment he thought he was going to pass out. His heart was beating so fast and loud that it sounded like a bass drum pounding in his ears. His thoughts raced through his head and none of them made sense. Jared had grown to hate the feeling of anxiety. Sadly he did not know how to stop feeling this way.

Anxiety causes many physical reactions that feel out of control. Did you know that anxiety has been associated with high blood pressure, headaches, and heart problems? Prolonged periods of exposure to anxiety sensations can even lead to premature death. But don't get discouraged; there is good news—the negative effects of anxiety are reversible and you hold the key to turning it around.

When you get these physical sensations it is your body's way of warning you that threats and danger exist. Often your body will start eliciting a response to an anxiety attack before it even happens. If you learn what your body's early warning signals are, you can fend off anxiety before it overwhelms you. One tool that you can use to detect anxiety is body scanning.

DIRECTIONS

It is super easy to do a body scan. Try this: pretend you are in a big machine that moves over your body when you are anxious. Every time the machine passes over a body part that shows stress it illuminates a red light. What red lights would be glowing on your body scan? For example, would it detect jaw constriction, rapid heartbeats, shoulder tension, headache? Many sensations could be going on at once so you may have multiple physical symptoms.

Go on and hop in the body scanner. Let it detect where you hold anxiety. On the diagram below write and color the areas you identified in red; this illustrates where your body illuminates stress and anxiety.

For example:

Head—if you experience headaches when stressed, you may color in red the part of the head where you feel the tension.

Torso—if your chest and neck break out in a rash when you get nervous, you may color your chest and neck red.

Head

_____

_____

Arms

_____

_____

Torso

_____

_____

Legs

_____

_____

Other

_____

_____

EXPAND ON IT

Answer the questions below:

1. From your body scan diagram, list an area of your body that is most affected by anxiety.

2. Describe the physical symptom you have that is most annoying.

3. List the early warning signs that your body gives to let you know that you are getting worked up.

4. Brainstorm and write down some ways that you could use your body scan to stop a full attack from occurring.

Did you know that you have more control over your body than you probably think? The next time you feel your body illuminating with anxiety take some deep breaths and focus on the things you listed to get yourself back in check with reality.

Activity 2.2

FIGHT OR FLIGHT

★

INTRODUCTION

When presented with a threat or danger you may go into a protected response called fight or flight. When this happens your body starts to release stress chemicals and hormones. The surge of chemicals causes your heart rate to increase, your breathing to become faster, your muscles to clench, and your blood vessels to constrict, reducing blood flow to the body. This physical reaction to stress is called the "fight or flight" response.

Fight or flight is your instinctive response to stress and anxiety. It occurs when you perceive something as a threat to your survival. When you feel in danger your body goes into action and takes over your mind. It begins to fight and protect you. Once your body is alert it asks you a question: "Do you want me to fight for you?" or "Do you want me to get out of this situation?" That is how it got its name *fight* or *flight*. Did you know that you can scare your body into a fight or flight reaction?

While fight or flight is a protection mechanism to keep you safe, you have the control to turn it on and off. It is not good when you activate it repeatedly because it can lead to major health problems such as high blood pressure, a suppressed immune system, heart problems, and stomach problems. So, if your fight or flight response is in overdrive it's time to stop turning it on all of the time and to start using it only for times when it needs to be activated.

Here are some things that may help you know when to activate the fight or flight response:

- Know your *mood*. If you're stressed out then try to avoid things that are worrisome.

- Know your *triggers*. Be able to identify things that make you anxious.

- Identify anxious *thoughts* and stop them from playing continuously in your head.

- Make a *decision* to handle the situation:

    a. Change your environment.

    b. Focus on the present.

    c. Put anxiety de-activation strategies in place.

- Recognize the *changes* that are happening in your body by doing a quick body scan.

DIRECTIONS

Read the two scenarios below. Answer the questions that follow.

Bethany's scenario—the big presentation

It was the day of Bethany's big presentation. She was so anxious, she hadn't slept for a week nor had she eaten much. She usually didn't have too much of an appetite when she was worked up. Beyond anything, Bethany hated speaking in front of crowds. She was so afraid that she would screw up or become the laughing stock of the school. But the big day had arrived and she had mustered the courage to do it.

When it was her turn she realized that she didn't have the most current version of her presentation. She felt sweat streaming down her face and she felt her cheeks burning with embarrassment. "I can't believe I did this," she thought. Bethany began to panic and couldn't think of what to do next. In the background she heard the whispering of her classmates. "I just know they are talking about me," she told herself. She heard the teacher prompt her to get started. Bethany freaked out and made a mad dash for the door!

Answer the following questions:

1. Describe the situation and Bethany's *mood* prior to the incident.

2. List the things that were *triggering* Bethany's anxiety.

3. Describe one of the anxious *thoughts* that Bethany had regarding the incident.

4. What *body* cues was Bethany's body giving to show she was anxious?

5. What could Bethany have done differently?

Trevor's scenario—the first day

Trevor's family had recently moved from a small town to the city. He didn't know anyone there and was forced to go to a much larger school. Trevor was a loner. He had a few friends back home and that was it. He didn't like getting to know new people or being around crowds. But now he didn't have a choice...

The first day of school rolled around and Trevor was already having thoughts of ditching it for the day. His mother dropped him off early that morning and he slowly made his way to his first class. He felt that all eyes were on him. Each thought he had played a negative message: "They are watching me. They are sizing me up. I don't belong here. I want to go home." Trevor felt his body reacting to the stress. He knew his neck and face had turned splotchy, as they always did when he was anxious. In the distance he saw the boys' bathroom and took off for it. "I'll just hide in here for the day," he thought.

1. Describe the situation and Trevor's *mood* prior to the incident.

2. List the things that were *triggering* Trevor's anxiety.

3. Describe one of the anxious *thoughts* that Trevor had regarding the incident.

4. What *body* cues was Trevor's body giving to show he was anxious?

5. What could Trevor have done differently?

EXPAND ON IT

Now it's your turn to describe a recent stressful situation you were in where your fight or flight response was activated.

Answer the following questions:

1. Describe the situation and your *mood* prior to the incident.

2. List the things that were *triggering* your anxiety.

3. Describe one of the anxious *thoughts* that you had regarding the incident.

4. List some cues your *body* was giving to indicate you were getting worked up.

5. Write a helpful action that you could take to make a better decision. What action would be unhelpful?

   a. Helpful Actions

   b. Unhelpful Actions

6. List some things that you could have done differently to produce a better outcome.

Activity 2.3

THE POWER OF A BREATH

INTRODUCTION

Breathing is the act of drawing air into and expelling it from the lungs. It is an involuntary and natural process that is vital to survival. Simply put, breathing is the difference between life and death and it plays a major role in coping with anxiety.

When you become stressed or anxious your breathing becomes shallow; the oxygen doesn't get to the brain as quickly, which causes stress and panic. Anxiety causes breathing to become short and more from the chest than from the abdomen. Abdominal breathing is the best kind of breathing because it enables oxygen to reach all of the vital organs, allowing your body to reap the full benefit of the breath. This type of breathing is the kind that you do when you are asleep. It's your body's natural and automatic way to breathe. If you don't know whether you do chest or abdominal breathing, try this...

Place one hand on your stomach and one on your chest. Breathe like you normally would. If your chest rises more than your abdomen then you're breathing with your chest. If your stomach rises fully then you're breathing with your abdomen—good job!

Breathing is a powerful thing. Did you know that proper breathing has lots of benefits? Proper breathing:

- increases energy levels

- increases your ability to focus and concentrate

- reduces muscle tension

- improves blood circulation

- improves your skin's appearance by releasing more carbon dioxide when you exhale

- helps you sleep better.

So, breathing is truly a wonderful anti-anxiety tool.

DIRECTIONS

Practice abdominal breathing. Here's what you'll need:

- a quiet setting that's free from distraction
- a comfortable flat surface like a floor.

Directions:

1. Lie flat on the floor.
2. Exhale all of the old air out of your body.
3. Place your hand on your abdomen.
4. Close your eyes and imagine having a balloon in your stomach that you have to blow up.
5. Take a deep breath through your nose slowly inflating your stomach. Remember, you're blowing up a balloon.
6. Next, imagine letting the air out of your balloon a little at a time and slowly exhale. You should feel your stomach getting flatter. Exhale until all of the air is released from your stomach.
7. Repeat this exercise over and over until you feel completely relaxed.

EXPAND ON IT

Over the next few hours pay special attention to your breathing. Are you breathing with your chest or your abdomen? If you find that air is going into your chest, change it to an abdominal breath. The more correctly you breathe, the better equipped you'll be to handle anxiety. Don't underestimate the power of a breath. It's a vital element to your very survival.

Activity 2.4

HEALTHY EATING

INTRODUCTION

Have you ever heard the saying "You are what you eat?" It means that what you put into your body has an effect on your mind and your body. Did you know that there are certain foods that make anxiety worse and some that can actually lessen it? In fact, if you're an anxious person you may find relief in changing your diet. Here are some culprits that may be responsible for triggering your anxiety: caffeine, alcohol, refined sugar, deficiency of B vitamins, calcium or magnesium, and food allergies.

We are all different, so some people may be more sensitive to certain foods than others. Take, for example, allergies; some people are deathly allergic to peanut butter while others can eat it by the spoonful. So food affects us differently, but science has shown us that what we eat can affect how we feel.

By eating foods that contain vitamins, amino acids, and complex carbohydrates you can increase chemicals in your brain that make you feel good, and believe it or not these foods also help you rest better at night. So do you want to know what these magic foods are? Read on and find out what foods are in your kitchen that may help you feel better.

Anxiety reducing foods contain:

- Complex carbohydrates—these act as sedatives by increasing serotonin in your brain. They help stabilize your blood sugar. You can find complex carbohydrates in wholewheat bread, grains, beans, brown rice, and fruit.

- Tryptophan—an amino acid that produces vitamin B3 and serotonin (the brain's mood-regulating hormone also called the "happy hormone"). Tryptophan is a compound found in turkey, shrimp, bananas, soy sauce, pumpkin seeds, and kale.

- Vitamin C—this has been shown to reduce stress hormones. Stress is a vitamin C destroyer. When your body is in stress mode it actually eats up levels of vitamin C in the adrenal glands. You probably think of oranges or citrus fruit when you think of vitamin C, but you can also get it from peaches, broccoli, eggs, spinach, and kiwi fruit.

- Omega-3 fatty acids—these are responsible for keeping cortisol (a stress hormone) balanced. If you like fish, then you're consuming Omega-3. But don't worry, if you don't like fish you can get it from nuts and soy beans.

Look at the healthy eating chart below. How many of these foods do you consume each day? Are you meeting your daily allowances?

Types of foods	Servings consumed
Vegetables	3–5 servings
Fruit	2–4 servings
Meats, poultry, fish, eggs, beans, nuts	2–3 servings
Milk, yogurt, cheese	2–3 servings
Grains, bread, cereal, rice, pasta	6–11 servings

Here are some quick tips to help you eat a more balanced diet:

- Eat lots of protein, fresh fruit, and vegetables.
- Limit junk food.
- Don't consume more than 100mg of caffeine each day. A can of fizzy drink has about 50–60mg per serving.
- Eat foods high in vitamins B and C.
- Watch your intake of refined and processed foods. A good way to see if it's refined or processed is to check out the ingredients. Here is a good rule of thumb—if it is not something your great grandmother would have cooked with then it's probably not good for you. When you get ready to grab a snack think of fresh, whole, and natural food—that's the best choice!

DIRECTIONS

How are your eating habits? For the next week record everything you eat in a food diary. Record the time, food/beverage, and your feeling/mood, before and after eating the item. Try to add some of the anxiety-reducing foods into your diet and eliminate those that make it worse.

Sunday	Time	Food/beverage	Feeling/mood Before and after
Monday	Time	Food/beverage	Feeling/mood Before and after
Tuesday	Time	Food/beverage	Feeling/mood Before and after
Wednesday	Time	Food/beverage	Feeling/mood Before and after

Thursday	Time	Food/beverage	Feeling/mood Before and after
Friday	Time	Food/beverage	Feeling/mood Before and after
Saturday	Time	Food/beverage	Feeling/mood Before and after

EXPAND ON IT

After one week, answer the following questions:

1. List any patterns you noticed in your eating habits. For example, did you drink a lot of tea or fizzy drinks or did you eat more when you were bored or stressed?

2. What time of day did you consume the most food?

3. What types of foods did you go for the most? For example, sweets, chips or fizzy drinks, or fruit and vegetables?

4. Look at how you felt before and after you ate the food. Describe any pattern that you observed before and after eating an item. For example were you stressed, agitated, bored, or nervous before you ate, or upset, sad, and disappointed after eating it?

5. Now that you have identified your weak areas, list some things that you can do to keep from eating things that aren't good for you. For example, list foods that you can substitute for healthy ones.

★

A food diary is a great tool to see your unhealthy eating habits. It can also help you become more conscientious about what you're eating and how it makes you feel. If all you have to do is change some of the things you're eating to feel better, isn't it worth the sacrifice?

EXERCISE

INTRODUCTION

One of the most powerful things you can do to reduce anxiety symptoms is to exercise. You don't have to be an athlete to exercise; anyone can do it. Just a simple walk, jog, or bike ride everyday would do the trick. Exercising is really about making a commitment to yourself and sticking to it.
    Just look at the wonderful things that exercise can do for you:

- improve mood

- increase strength

- help maintain or lose weight

- reduce the risk of cancer

- improve blood pressure

- decrease symptoms of depression

- decrease symptoms of anxiety

- reduce tension

- increase memory performance

- improve flexibility

- decrease chances of heart disease

- increase self-confidence

- improve body image

...and the list goes on and on.

DIRECTIONS

Look at the list of activities and circle any that you enjoy or want to try. There's room at the end for you to add others that you're interested in doing.

Aerobics	Archery	Badminton	Baseball
Basketball	Bowling	Boxing	Cheerleading
Cycling	Dancing	Diving	Football
Frisbee	Golf	Gymnastics	Hiking
Hockey	Horseback riding	Kayaking	Lacrosse
Longboarding	Martial arts	Paddle surfing	Racquetball
Rock rappelling	Rope jumping	Running	Skateboarding
Skating	Skiing	Soccer	Softball
Surfing	Swimming	Tennis	Volleyball
Walking	Weight training	Yoga	
Other:	_____	_____	_____

What activities do you enjoy doing or would be willing to try?

How much time can you commit to exercising each week?

What days work best with your schedule?

What is the best time of day for you to fit an activity into your schedule?

Make a game plan to exercise next week and use the activity log in the next section to help you stick to your plan.

EXPAND ON IT

★ For the next week make a commitment to fit exercise into your schedule. Use the activity log to help you keep track of your progress and moods. Pay special attention to how you feel after you exercise.

Day	Time	Activity	Feeling before activity	Feeling after activity
Sunday				
Monday				
Tuesday				
Wednesday				
Thursday				
Friday				
Saturday				

Activity 2.6

A GOOD NIGHT'S REST

★

INTRODUCTION

Sleep is your body's way of recuperating and resting. Your body needs Zzzs to function and operate. Just as healthy eating and exercising are vital to your health, so is sleep. On average a person your age needs between seven and nine hours of consistent sleep each night. Are you getting enough sleep? If not, there is a whole host of problems that can occur, such as feeling drained, being more susceptible to illness, not being able to concentrate, and so on... Some people even turn to using drugs when they don't get enough sleep. There is no way around it: you need sleep to function and cope.

Emma's alarm echoed across the room. "Just a little longer," Emma thought. She reached groggily across to her nightstand, picked up her phone and silenced the annoying sound. It was 5:30am and Emma had another busy day awaiting her, but like most mornings she woke up feeling as if she hadn't slept at all. With everything Emma had on her plate, she was lucky to get five hours of sleep a night...and it was catching up with her. The bags under her eyes and her mood swings were all indicators of fatigue.

Emma raced downstairs to eat her bowl of cereal and down a glass of orange juice before heading to school. As she rounded the corner to the kitchen, her mother stopped and looked at her. "Emma," she said, "you look horrible." "Gee, thanks," Emma responded. Her mother shook her head, "I didn't mean it like that... I am really getting worried about you. Why don't you stay at home today and rest?" Emma thought of everything she had on her plate and said, "I can't. I have too much to do." "Emma," her mother replied, "if you don't take care of yourself you're not going to be able to do anything well. Trust me on this. I promise, after some rest, things will become clearer and you'll feel better. Everything else comes second to your health and well-being." Emma thought about it and succumbed to her mother's advice. "Okay, Mom, I guess one day won't hurt," she said. Besides, the thought of laying her head back down on the pillow sounded pretty good.

Later that morning when Emma woke up, she and her mother spent some time designing a sleep schedule. Here are some things they came up with:

- Set a regular bedtime schedule and stick to it. Emma wanted to make sure she got at least eight hours of sleep a night.

  Emma said that she'd be in bed between 9:30 pm and 10:00 pm.

- Get up around the same time each day.

  On school days Emma decided to wake up at 6:30 am.

- Be sure to get physical exercise during the day.

  Emma played a sport, so she had practice each day after school, which gave her an outlet to stay fit.

- Keep distractions out of the room; for example, mobile phones, laptops, tablets, televisions, etc. A bedroom should be a relaxing environment and a place that's anxiety free.

  Emma removed all of her electronic devices from her room so that she would not wake up and be tempted to use them in the middle of the night.

- Eat healthily. Avoid stimulating foods high in carbohydrates and caffeine.

  Emma realized that eating her favorite chocolate ice cream with chocolate syrup wasn't the best idea before bedtime. The sugar and caffeine were probably contributing to her restlessness.

- Set up a night time ritual.

  Emma wrote down the following rituals to put in place each night before she went to bed.

  - Read a chapter in a book or magazine for pleasure before bed.

  - Take a warm bath, but not too hot because that will increase body temperature making it difficult to fall asleep.

  - Listen to music.

  - Do some relaxation exercise or meditate before bed.

  - Take a powernap after school. A 30-minute nap (or even less) can recharge your battery!

Emma felt that the schedule she and her mother designed was doable and the thought of rest sounded so good she went back to bed and took another nap.

DIRECTIONS

Like Emma, make your own sleep schedule, starting by answering the following questions:

1. How do you feel when you are tired?

2. How do you behave when you are tired?

3. On average how many hours of sleep do you get each night?

4. Make your own sleep schedule.

Here are some tips:

1. Set a regular bedtime and stick to it.

2. Get up the same time each day.

3. Be sure to get physical exercise during the day.

4. Keep distractions out of your room; for example, mobile phones, laptops, tablets, televisions, etc. Your room should be a relaxing environment and place that's anxiety free.

5. Keep your room dark at night.

6. Eat healthily. Avoid stimulating foods high in carbohydrates and caffeine.

7. Set up a night time ritual.

EXPAND ON IT

Make a Zzzs schedule. Each day record how you felt that day. See if you notice a pattern in your mood on days when you get enough rest and days when you do not sleep enough.

Zzzs schedule

Day	Time to bed	Time awake	Nap	Sleep total	How you feel
Sunday					
Monday					
Tuesday					
Wednesday					
Thursday					
Friday					
Saturday					

Activity 2.7

FIT FOR LIFE

INTRODUCTION

Fit for life means being healthy and taking care of yourself both on the inside and out. There are countless benefits associated with being fit. Choosing to be "fit for life" can help increase energy, mental focus, and self-esteem, while decreasing stress and anxiety. Your overall mood will improve if you're healthy and in shape.

Taking care of your body is extremely important in the battle against anxiety. Not only is exercise a terrific physical outlet, it also helps with mental alertness. It makes you able to think more clearly by releasing all of the negative stuff that's loading you down. Being fit for life is a choice, a choice that will only make you feel better. Just look at what anxiety does compared with the benefits of being fit.

Anxiety negatively affects:

- sleep

- appetite

- work/academic performance

- energy levels

- confidence

- motivation.

Being fit:

- promotes better sleep

- helps improve your mood

- boosts energy

- reverses the detrimental effects of stress

- improves your health

- improves learning

- helps combat depression

- helps increase self-confidence

- improves body image.

So, what are you going to do? Let anxiety eat away at you or get fit for life?

DIRECTIONS

Start getting fit for life by making a commitment to yourself. Read each tip below and commit to getting fit.

1. Get out of your comfort zone. Doing something you wouldn't normally do. Remember you have goals to reach and values to live by. You are in training to reach them. The sky is the limit, so think big and do something you have never done before. Examples may include running in a race or whitewater rafting. At least once a month participate in an activity that is safe, but completely out of your comfort zone.

List something that is doable that you have always wanted to do, but haven't.

What's keeping you from doing it?

In the space below make a plan to do it.

When is your goal to having accomplished it?

2. Do some kind of activity every day. It's good to alternate between cardiovascular exercise and some type of resistance exercise. So one day go for a 30-minute power walk, and the next day do something else physical that you enjoy.

For the next week do an activity every day and record in the space below:

Sunday

Monday

Tuesday

Wednesday

Thursday

Friday

Saturday

★

3. Play a sport. Even adults enjoy playing sports. It doesn't matter if you are good or not, just get out there with your school or club team and give it all you've got.

What sport do you play?

If you don't play a sport, which one will you try?

4. Eat nutritious foods every three to four hours. Eating small healthy meals frequently throughout the day helps provide a consistent supply of energy and helps your body become fit.

Do you skip meals?

List healthy foods that you eat often.

List unhealthy foods that you eat often.

List what you would eat in a typical day:

Breakfast	Lunch	Dinner	Snacks	Beverages

Are most of the foods you eat unhealthy or healthy?

For the next week, substitute one of your unhealthy food choices for a healthy one.

5. Provide your body with lots of rest. If you're not getting seven to nine hours of sleep each night you are significantly limiting your ability to lose body fat and develop lean muscle. Not getting enough sleep will cause a stress response in your body and raise cortisol hormone levels. This will make it very difficult to release stored body fat and allow for muscle regrowth and recovery. Many teens have trouble getting enough rest, so this is a very important one.

How much sleep do you get on average each night?

Is your sleep a rested one or do you wake up a lot during the night?

For the next week get between seven and nine hours of sleep each night.

EXPAND ON IT

For the course of the next week keep a fit for life log. Pay special attention to the amount of sleep that you get each day, eating habits, and exercise. If you notice problem areas, work on fixing them. The more fit you become the better you will feel.

Day	Sleep hours	Unhealthy foods	Healthy foods	Exercise
Sunday				
Monday				
Tuesday				
Wednesday				
Thursday				
Friday				
Saturday				

MINDFULNESS AND THE BODY

INTRODUCTION

Have you ever picked up a shell on the beach and put it to your ear? Did you hear the ocean? Odds are you probably had to block out distractions and background noise to hear the sound of the ocean waves amplifying through the shell. Okay, you know it wasn't the real ocean you were hearing, as the shells just make great amplifiers of surrounding noises. But in order to hear what sounded like waves crashing on the beach, you had to shut out the background noise. This ability to focus on the here and now is called mindfulness. Mindfulness is being aware and fully present in the moment you are living in. Often people get so busy thinking about what's going to happen in the future that they forget to pay attention to what is happening right now. Learning to shut out the background noise is a great way to work through anxiety.

DIRECTIONS

Practice being mindful and shutting out all of the background noise. For this activity you will put all your time and energy into focusing on the activity. Before you get started you'll need a quiet location that's free from distractions and a piece of fruit of your choice.

1. Get in a comfortable position (you can lie flat if you like). Like listening to a seashell, try to block out distractions. Let your thoughts come and go, like waves in the ocean. Don't spend time focusing on anything except where you are: right here, right now.

2. Practice abdominal breathing. Let the air fill your lungs, and feel your abdomen rise and fall with each breath. Take a couple of these breaths.

3. Next, sit up if you're lying down and take a bite of the fruit you chose. Chew slowly. Focus on the taste, texture, sweetness, smell, and juiciness. Let the flavor fill your mouth. Enjoy each bite and focus only on the fruit. If your mind begins to wander, it is okay; just bring it back to the fruit and its flavor.

4. Once you finish your fruit, take some time to stretch your muscles. Notice their tightness, feel the pull of the stretch. Release and repeat. Notice how your muscles feel after being stretched.

5. Finish this activity with another round of abdominal breathing. You should feel completely relaxed and in tune with how your body is feeling by now.

Congratulations! You just did your first activity in mindfulness. How often do you shut out the background noise and focus solely on what you are doing?

EXPAND ON IT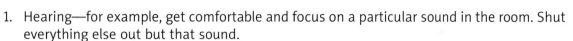

Practice mindfulness. When you practice use your five basic senses:

1. Hearing—for example, get comfortable and focus on a particular sound in the room. Shut everything else out but that sound.

2. Seeing—hold something special in your hand and spend time just studying each intricate detail of the object. Block out all other distractions except what you are holding.

3. Smelling—focus on a pleasant smell. Close your eyes and just let that aroma consume you.

4. Touching—get something with nice texture such as velvet, cotton, smooth glass, etc. Close your eyes and hold the object in your hands; focus only on feeling and studying the object. Is it silky, soft, rough, etc.?

5. Tasting—try this same activity with another food item such as raisins, pretzels, or chocolate.

Chapter Three

ANXIETY AND THOUGHTS

The way we think affects how we feel and the way we feel determines how we act. In order to change how we act, we must first work on our thoughts.

Chapter outline

Chapter objectives

From this chapter you will:

- learn how negative thoughts can be defeating

- explore thought patterns that can cause more anxiety

- learn how to separate your thoughts from who you are

- understand that a thought is just a thought

- explore ways to find solutions to your problems

- learn to let go of harmful thoughts.

Pre-/post-scaling questions

Pre-question

On a scale of 0 to 10, with zero being "a little" and 10 being "a lot," rate how often you engage in negative and self-defeating thinking. For example, do you call yourself bad names? Do you replay bad thoughts and experiences over and over again in your head? Plot the score on the grid below.

Post-question

Okay, it is hoped that you've had a chance to explore those negative words and thoughts that you tell yourself. At the beginning of this chapter you rated yourself at a _____ (let them know the pre-score rating) for how often you engage in negative thinking. Using the same scale of 0 to 10, with zero being "a little" and 10 being "a lot," rate where you are now in understanding your negative thoughts. Plot the post-score on the grid below.

Here are some samply follow-up questions that can assist you in comparing and contrasting your client's score:

- "I noticed that you moved from a '4' to a '6' on the scale. What are some things that contributed to you moving up?"

- "What are some things that you can do to help you move closer to a '10?'"

- "Are there any things that you feel you'd like to work on more in this chapter that would help you move up on the scale?"

- "I noticed that you moved down or stayed the same on the scale. What are some things that you can do to help you move up on the scale?"

- "What are some things that can help you move up on the scale?"

- "What was the most helpful thing that you learned?"

- "What did you find not useful at all?"

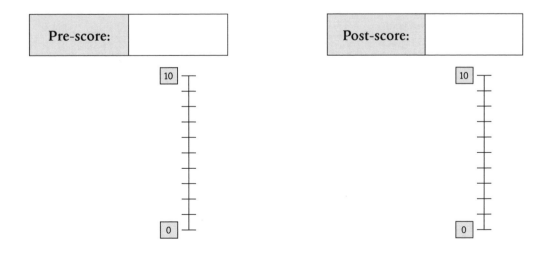

Activity 3.1

THOUGHT DEFUSION

★

INTRODUCTION

Sara had trouble sleeping. Her thoughts were racing through her mind and she lay in bed in a cold sweat. She had tried counting sheep...she had heard that from somewhere, but it didn't work. Her struggle with sleep had been going on for a while now and it was getting old. Sara got out of her bed and made her way downstairs. She noticed a light coming from the family room. "I must not be the only one up," she thought. She walked into the room and noticed her dad in the corner working on his computer. "Can't sleep?" he asked. She told him that she had a lot on her mind and couldn't get settled. "I guess it's the anxiety getting to me," she told him. To her surprise her dad confessed that he too struggled with high levels of stress that sometimes caused him to lose sleep. His symptoms mirrored hers to a tee.

Sara asked him if he had any solutions to help her sleep. Her dad shared with her his special secret to calming an anxious mind and getting a good night's rest; counting sheep wasn't one of them. Her dad showed her something called "thought defusion." He said, "It doesn't make the feeling disappear immediately but it helps remind you that your thoughts are separate from you as a person." Then he said something that made a lot of sense, "Thoughts are random and unpredictable; they come and they go. What you are worrying about today may not be a big deal tomorrow."

Curious, Sara asked him to show her the thought-defusing exercise. "Sure, here's how it works. First, draw a large circle and write the situation that is troubling you in the circle. Then on the outside of the circle write all of the anxious thoughts that your are having and draw circles round your thoughts. Once that's done connect all of your thought circles to your problem with lines. On the lines write the statement 'I am having the thought...' This helps show you that everything you're worrying about is not really who you are but a thought that you are having. Thoughts are like words scrolling across the bottom of a television screen. Let them scroll on by, don't hold onto them. Think of it as if you're watching your thoughts from the outside looking in and then they won't seem so big."

Sara took a piece of paper and did her own thought-defusion activity. In the center of the circle she wrote: *Broke up with boyfriend and the jerk is spreading nasty and hurtful rumors about me.*

In the surrounding circles she wrote:

- No one likes me.

- I am going to be lonely.

- I am ugly.

- Everyone's talking about me.

- What if he tells the things I told him in confidence? He's ruined my life.

She wrote "I am having the thought…" on each line. Then Sara circled the thought that was causing her a lot of anxiety. One of her biggest fears was "What if he tells the things I told him in confidence?" Sara realized that was the big one that was keeping her up at night. She also realized that her thoughts were causing her fear and anxiety to escalate. Her dad was right, they were just thoughts. After this activity, Sara realized how separate her thoughts really were from her as a person and how all that she needed to worry about was the present, right here, right now.

DIRECTIONS

Thoughts are ideas, memories, and predictions that are sparked from deep within our conscious. We are constantly thinking about something, and sometimes multiple things at once. Thoughts typically come and go, but when we get hung up on them they can become problematic, especially if they aren't healthy ones. You can learn to let your thoughts come and go, and not get hooked on them. The more you fight your feelings, the more they control you.

Like Sara, give thought diffusion a try. In the large circle write down the situation that you are thinking about. In the circles surrounding the situation write your anxious thoughts. Next connect the small thought circles to the situation circle by drawing lines. On the lines write the statement "I am having the thought…"

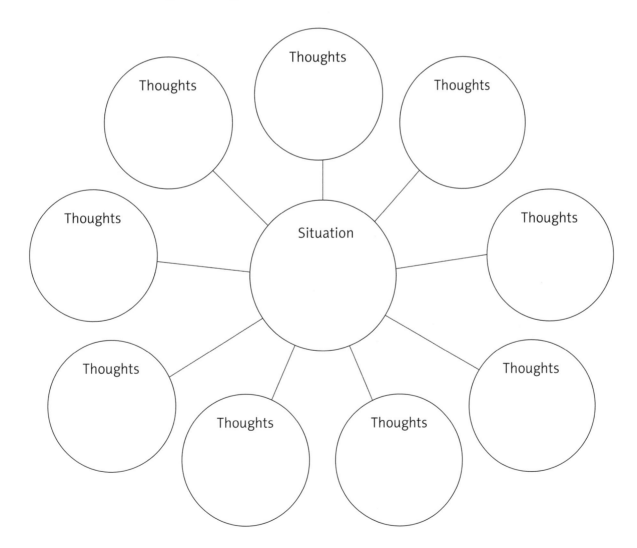

EXPAND ON IT

★ Questions

1. Describe what it was like to stand apart from your thoughts.

2. Describe any pattern or theme that your thoughts followed.

3. Take a few small pieces of paper or sticky notes and write the words, "I am having the thought…" Next time you find your thoughts are running away from you remind yourself that it's just a thought. After you write down your thoughts take the papers and discard them. They are only thoughts and hold no power over you.

Activity 3.2

PERCEPTION

INTRODUCTION

Isn't it amazing how two people can be involved in the same situation, but have very different takes on it? Take for example, Mark who has agoraphobia and is very fearful of going outside because he is afraid that something will happen to him, but in reality he is no more at risk of something happening than any of the other millions of people who go outside every day. So what makes Mark's situation different? The answer lies in his perception of what he thinks will happen to him. Perception is his reality. Perception is how we see the world around us, and, more importantly, how we respond to it depends on our perception of what's going on. Perception and anxiety go hand in hand. How you perceive an event triggers your anxiety, but are you seeing the full picture?

DIRECTIONS

Everything that we visually take in is filtered through our perceptual lens. Our world is shaped by what we see. Our perception offers one way of seeing a situation; however, often there is more than one way to see something. Take, for example, Mark's situation. He's fearful of going outside based on his perception that something will happen to him. Now compare that to another person, who is walking outside right now without any fear or anxiety of something happening. This person's perception of going outside is completely different from Mark's. There are usually multiple ways to see something, and multiple solutions. To help illustrate this lesson let's play with perception. Look at the following pictures.

What do you see in this picture?

Do you see an old woman or a young woman? They're both there. Do you see the profile of a young lady wearing a stole and a fancy hat with a plume? Still can't see it? She's looking to her right. Now try to see the elderly lady who has a stoic, yet sad, expression. She is looking down, and the young woman's chin is the bottom of her nose. Which one stands out the most—the young lady or the elderly woman?

Your mind sees one image more clearly than the other, but you can flip between the two. With practice you can learn to understand people by flipping around your perception of what's really happening.

Here's another example for you. What do you see in this picture?

This illustration provides a picture of a boy and his father. Can you see both? Look closely, the father is looking towards the right and his chin is resting on his chest. The father is wearing an old tethered hat. The son is looking over his left shoulder. Can you see him? If not, take a look at the father's nose and imagine it being a chin. The nose is the chin of the son and the son is wearing a cavalier style hat.

If someone sees the opposite to you would that make them wrong or is either way right? Now, think of a time in your life where you let anxiety skew your perception. Odds are you let your perception drive your actions. By stepping back to make sure you see the whole picture and aren't missing any details, you can not only decrease stress, but you can change your reactions in an anxiety-provoking situation.

Want to play more perception games? The internet has hundreds and thousands of fun optical illusions and perception games. All you need to do is search the key words 'optical illusion' and you'll find some great ways to practice seeing things differently.

EXPAND ON IT

Try this...

Put your hand right in front of your face: what do you see? Now move your hand at an arm's length: what do you see? Do you see more detail, or things in the background? Sometimes when we're in a conflict we only see what's directly in front of our face rather than the whole picture. Anxiety has a tendency to keep us focused on only what's directly in front of our face and not on the big picture. It also alters our perception so we see only what we want to see.

Activity 3.3

DISTORTIONS

INTRODUCTION

Imagine looking at your reflection in a pond of still, crystal clear water. Now imagine picking up a rock and tossing it in the water. What happens? Your reflection becomes distorted or altered by the ripples and waves in the water, so while the reflection is still you it is altered by the waves. Similar to casting a stone into still water, anxiety can alter reality so the situation gets taken out of context and reality becomes distorted. When this happens you may not see the situation crystal clear any longer. Reacting on distorted perceptions can be a slippery slope because you don't have the complete picture of what is happening. So it's best to wait until the water is calm before reacting.

When your thoughts become distorted it is difficult to separate reality from fiction. You can learn to identify when you are casting a stone into a situation. In fact, there are several different types of "stones," referred to as distortions. When you fling a distortion into a situation, the image and perception become altered. Worst still, when you react to a distorted perception you can get into a lot of trouble, because it's not reality. Realizing when things are distorted and what stone (distortion) you're throwing is an important step in learning to keep the water still and calm.

DIRECTIONS

Take the quiz below by answering "yes" or "no."

1. Have you ever assumed the worst in a situation and felt that no matter what you did it was hopeless?

2. Have you ever done something and then gone back and picked apart all of your mistakes, failing to see what you did right?

3. Have you ever made a mistake and then felt like a complete failure?

4. Have you ever made a situation far bigger than it really was?

5. Have you ever called yourself bad names such as *loser, failure, screw-up,* etc.?

6. Have you ever blamed yourself for things that weren't your fault?

7. Have you ever jumped to a conclusion, usually the worst one, without having enough information?

8. Have you ever had a bad experience and because of it felt that it would happen forevermore?

Score: How many "yeses" did you get? Each question represented a type of distortion. Look at the examples of cognitive distortions below and go back to write the distortion that was used in each question above. The answers are listed at the end of this activity.

Types of cognitive distortions

Catastrophizing (1)

Do you automatically assume the worst possible outcome? Do you feel as if the world is going to end when something goes wrong? How often do you use statements such as "This is the worst day of my life" or "I can't ever show my face in public again!"?

Diminishing the positives (2)

Having trouble accepting compliments for a job well done? That's what happens when you diminish the positives in your life, you let negativism invade your life and discount the good.

All or nothing (3)

Do you believe that your way is the only right way of doing things? If it's not done your way then it's not good enough. Absolute thinking often has words such as "never," "always," and "every" in the statements. For example, "I'm always last," "This happens every time" or "I never do anything right."

Maximizing (4)

This is blowing things out of proportion and making them bigger than they really are. Some people use the phrase "making a mountain out of a mole hill" to describe this type of distortion.

Labeling (5)

This distortion is calling yourself names and putting yourself down. For example, calling yourself a "failure," "loser," "idiot," or feeling as if you'll "never be anything."

Personalization (6)

Personalization is assuming responsibility for things that are outside your control. So, you take everything bad personally. For example, you may feel "It's my fault my friend didn't get to have the sleep over," or "It's all my fault the group got a bad grade."

Jumping to conclusions (7)

Jumping to conclusions is drawing conclusions without any evidence to support your interpretation.

Overgeneralization (8)

Overgeneralization is taking a negative experience and expecting it to keep happening. For example, a person who uses overgeneralization may feel that because she didn't have any friends in middle school, she won't have any in high school either, or because he didn't make the basketball team this year, he won't make it the next, so why try?

EXPAND ON IT

Challenge it! Learn to challenge your distortions. Look at the challenges below and complete the activity that follows.

Types of cognitive distortions

Diminishing the positives—challenge it

Go ahead and accept the positives in your life. Be proud of what you accomplish. Rather than discrediting your work, think "I am a hard worker" or "I deserved that." If you accept the positives it will not only help you feel better but it will also boost your confidence!

All or nothing—challenge it

Absolute thinking will set you up for disappointment because you are setting unrealistic expectations. Remember, there are few situations in life that are absolute. If you catch yourself using absolute thinking, challenge it!

Catastrophizing—challenge it

Ask yourself, "Is it really the worst day of my life as opposed to just a really bad day?" Sure, it may feel as though you can't show your face in public, but the reality is it's just an embarrassing moment that will pass. Remember, it is one bad situation, not your whole life.

Jumping to conclusions—challenge it

Put on your investigator hat if you find yourself engaging in this type of thinking. Ask yourself, "Do I have enough information to assume this or is it just how I feel?" If you determine you've jumped to a conclusion without enough evidence then focus on facts not assumptions.

Labeling—challenge it

Every negative has a positive. Often after a disappointing event we may feel like we aren't good at anything, but the reality is we just made a mistake. Mistakes are going to happen, but if you bash yourself every time you make one then you're only going to feel worse. Challenge self-defeating talk by substituting it for more positive talk.

Overgeneralization—challenge it

Negative things are going to happen. Accept it for what it is—a negative event—and don't let it predict your future. You can take negative events and create different outcomes. For example, if you didn't have friends in middle school then get involved in clubs or other activities to meet more people in high school. If you didn't do well on a test then study harder, stay after school with the teacher before the test, or join a study group so you'll do better on the next one.

Personalization—challenge it

When we personalize things we take full responsibility for the situation. Evaluate situations to determine whether you have any responsibility for the outcome. Remember, you are not responsible for other people's decisions or actions.

Maximizing—challenge it

Think logically through the situation. Are you making a bigger deal out of it than you need to? If so, then stop and think through the situation. Sometimes it's good to bounce things off someone else who may have a different perspective to you and can help keep you grounded in reality.

Take the challenge and write out a positive message for each distorted statement. Next write some of your own distortions and challenge them.

1. Everyone got invited but me. I'm such a loser.

   Challenge it:

2. This is the worst day of my life. I'll never be able to show my face again.

   Challenge it:

3. I can't do anything right.

   Challenge it:

4. That spider is going to bite me and I'll die.

   Challenge it:

5. She never called me. She must not like me anymore.

   Challenge it:

6. _____.

   Challenge it:

7. _____.

   Challenge it:

8. _____.

   Challenge it:

9. _____.

   Challenge it:

10. _____.

    Challenge it:

Answers to the quiz

Catastrophizing (1)

Diminishing the positives (2)

All or nothing (3)

Maximizing (4)

Labeling (5)

Personalization (6)

Jumping to conclusions (7)

Overgeneralization (8)

Activity 3.4

ABSOLUTES

INTRODUCTION

Eli was a 17-year-old teen with anxiety. He had an extreme fear of being around other people. He frequently tortured himself with thoughts of "always screwing up" or "mispronouncing words" in front of others. Eli felt as though everyone was either talking about him or laughing at him. The last time he tried to hang out with some people he made a complete fool of himself and people talked about him for weeks. Eli just knew it would happen again.

Eli was very hard on himself. He had extremely high expectations and when he didn't meet them, he would beat himself up repeatedly. In fact, Eli was his own worst enemy. He saw things in black and white. If he wasn't successful then he thought he was a failure. If he embarrassed himself, then he avoided trying the very thing that embarrassed him again, because he was certain history would repeat itself. Eli's concrete and rigid thinking style was like living in a world without mistakes and one that was sure to bring disappointment.

Eli's type of hurtful and negative thinking is referred to as "absolute thinking." By definition, absolute means being perfect and pure—an impossible characteristic for any human to achieve. Absolute thinking is seeing things in black and white terms. Trigger words such as *never, should, always,* and *everyone* are absolute words that you probably use in your everyday language without realizing how often you use them. Absolute words set up false beliefs of perfectionism, and no one is perfect. In fact, few things in life are absolute.

DIRECTIONS

Take a look at the table below. The left side shows phrases that are absolutes; the right side shows more realistic words. The next time you find yourself engaging in absolute thinking, exchange those words for the ones on the right side.

When thinking this:	Try thinking this:
I must...	I would like to...
I should...	I prefer...
I have to...	I choose to
I can't...	I choose not to...
I need...	I would like...
I never...	I sometimes...

110

When thinking this:	Try thinking this:
I always...	I often...
I am a failure...	I didn't do well at...
I am a bad person...	I made a poor decision...

Challenge absolute thinking by rewriting the thoughts below.

When thinking this...   Try thinking this...

1. This is a *total* disaster!

2. I *always* get blamed for everything!

3. It's *always* my fault!

4. I can *never* trust anyone!

5. I *must* get into that school!

6. I *have* to do it my way!

7. I'm *always* wrong!

8. I *know* that they are talking about me.

9. Why does *everyone* pick on me?

10. *Everything's* ruined!

11. I *can't* walk in there alone.

12. I *won't* be able to do it!

13. _____

14. _____

15. _____

16. _____

17. _____

18. _____

19. _____

20. _____

EXPAND ON IT

Pay attention to how often you use absolute vocabulary and also how often others use it. Once you start noticing it you will see how limiting it can be. Keep a tally record for a day of how often you use absolute words.

Absolute terms	Tally marks
Everyone	
Everything	
Must	
Should	
Can't	
Never	
Always	
Only	
All	
None	

THOUGHT BASHING

INTRODUCTION

Have you ever noticed that it is easier to dish out advice than take it? Why is that? One reason may be because when you're on the outside looking in it's easier to see which direction someone should take, but when you're in the middle of a crisis it's not so clear which path to take. Often, when in a crisis you may come down really hard on yourself and put yourself down for not handling something right. But if you were helping another person find the right path would you be saying the same things to them that you say to yourself or would you be more encouraging and uplifting?

Think about it, would you say some of the things you say to yourself to a friend? Would you call your friend stupid? Worthless? A failure? Good for nothing? A moron? An idiot? Odds are you wouldn't. So why do you do it to yourself? When you think bad things about yourself you're engaging in something called thought bashing. One way to fix your negative thoughts is to replace them rather than resist them. While you are at it, replace them with more positive ones. Here is a basic rule for you to follow—if you wouldn't say what you're thinking to a friend, don't say it to yourself.

DIRECTIONS

The picture on the next page is a new friend to you who struggles with anxiety just like you. So, go ahead and give your friend a name.

Name of friend: _____

You like your friend so much that you don't want him/her to go through the same things that you struggle with. In the blank quotation boxes write some negative thoughts that your friend has about himself/herself. In the boxes below your friend's thoughts write the advice you'd give your friend about that thought.

★

EXPAND ON IT

1. List how you can take your own advice and challenge your own thoughts.

2. Write a negative thought that haunts you the most about yourself.

3. If one of your close friends had that thought what advice would you give him/her?

Activity 3.6

FINDING SOLUTIONS

★

INTRODUCTION

Good problem solving involves thinking through and playing out various situations in your head. It is also about changing a belief that a problem is too big to handle into a belief that you can find a solution to your problems. In order to resolve a problem, you must first define it, explore how it is affecting you, and then think of ways to solve it.

Each time Mandy went into Mr. Swanson's biology class she felt sick to her stomach. In fact, she hated going to his class so much that she would create any excuse just to miss it. One of the reasons Mandy hated his class was because he had an oral-speaking component built into his grading system. That meant he required his students to speak out and contribute to class to earn points toward their grade. The thought of having to speak in public made Mandy clam up and feel sick. It was no surprise that Mandy was failing Mr. Swanson's class.

A month ago, she had started seeing a counselor for anxiety. While she was beginning to learn coping skills, she still had a long way to go. One day Mandy mentioned Mr. Swanson's class to her therapist. "Mandy," her therapist said, "have you ever spoken to Mr. Swanson about how you feel in his class?" Mandy thought for a few seconds "No," she replied. "Well… it may be a good idea to speak with him. I bet if he knew what was going on he'd be more able to work with you. Plus, your performance in his class will start to improve. Isn't it worth a try, I mean what do you have to lose? What might you have to gain?" Mandy thought about it and then said, "I guess I have nothing to lose." "That's right, Mandy," her therapist replied. "One of the goals in therapy is taking an anxiety-producing situation and searching for some solutions. Let's work through a plan to help you find your own solution."

Mandy's problem seems really big to her, but if she breaks it down it may feel more manageable. Here are the steps Mandy and her counselor worked through to find a solution:

1. Define the problem.

    Teacher requires students to speak in class and grades them for their contributions. I am afraid of speaking in front of other people.

2. List how the problem is affecting you.

    Avoiding class, getting sick, and failing grade.

3. Possible solutions.

    Have a parent–teacher conference.

    Speak with the teacher.

    Arrange an alternative assignment rather than speaking in front of the class.

    Pursue a teacher change, if things don't improve.

After working through this activity, Mandy felt more in control. In the past she had tried to avoid what was troubling her and push it out of her mind. Unfortunately, this approach wasn't working because the situation still existed, it never went away... This new approach required her to face her fear, but find an acceptable way to deal with it.

DIRECTIONS

Using the problem-solving method above can you help Chris work through his problem?

Chris was in his final year of high school. While he was excited about his final year the thought of leaving school triggered his anxiety. He was extremely afraid of the unknown and what would happen after high school. Chris had been accepted by two universities and as his school graduation date approached, he found that rather than celebrating he felt nauseous, had migraines, and his grades were slipping. Chris felt as if something was wrong with him, but he hadn't spoken to anyone about his fears. Can you help him find a solution, so he doesn't have to feel this way?

1. Define Chris' problem.

2. List how the problem is affecting Chris.

3. Find possible solutions for Chris.

EXPAND ON IT

Now it's your turn to write down your own situation and then work through the problem-solving method. You hold the key to your own answers. Give it a try.

Situation:

1. Define your problem.

2. List how the problem is affecting you.

3. Find possible solutions.

Revisit this page when you try your solutions. Write about what changed when you put your solutions into place.

DECISIONAL BALANCING

★

INTRODUCTION

Life can throw some difficult situations your way that require you to make a quick decision. That decision may not be an easy one and it may cause apprehension and anxiety. When you are faced with a stressful decision you don't have to let it dominate your life. Stress can keep you from exploring all your options. That's why it's important to collect all your information before you react hastily. One way to do this is by using decisional balancing.

Chase is a 14-year-old boy who is struggling with a lot of stress and anxiety. His anxiety feels as if it's suffocating him. He just can't shake it and it frequently consumes him. One of the things that has been stressing Chase out lately is his parents' nasty divorce. They are making him choose who to live with. While Chase gets along with both his parents, there are some other factors that make his decision a harder one to make.

Chase loves both his mother and father and wishes he didn't have to make this decision... But his father is planning to move out of town. So to live with him would mean leaving his friends behind. Due to all the pressure this decision is causing, Chase is constantly on edge and freaks out about every little thing. The stress has caused other problems too... Chase hasn't slept well in months and his grades have slipped. He has even lost weight because this decision making is too much for him to bear. Who does he turn to? Chase has some tough decisions to make because this isn't going away until he decides what to do.

Chase is going to need to make a decision and either way someone is going to be hurt. Sometimes life decisions are difficult to make. Decisional balancing is a tool that you can use to help you find the best option. Let's walk Chase through decisional balancing.

Chase's decision: live with Mom or Dad?

Pros with Mom	Cons with Mom
• I won't have to move away from my friends • I won't have to change houses • I can go to the same school • Life would be like it is now, only Dad wouldn't be there	• I'll miss Dad • Mom has more rules than Dad
Pros with Dad	**Cons with Dad**
• I get along with Dad • I'll have more freedom	• I'll miss Mom • I'll have to move • I'll have to make new friends • I'll have to change schools

Balance the decision...Which option is the best?

It looks like the best option would be to live with Mom. Even though this is not a decision anyone wants to make, in this case it has to be made. Decisional balancing is a helpful way to make the decision more manageable.

DIRECTIONS

Sometimes life can throw some difficult decisions your way and you may not know what to do. When this happens you can narrow down your options by doing your own decisional balancing. Some decisions only have one option, while others are more complex, like Chase's. Regardless of whether your decision has one option or more, you can use decisional balancing to help you sort through the pros and cons of each option.

Think of a difficult decision that you are currently facing or have recently faced. Just like Chase, work through the options of your decision. If your decision only has one option, only fill in one box.

My decision

Option A:

Pros	Cons

Option B:

Pros	Cons

Balance the decision... Which option is the best?

_____

_____

_____

_____

_____

EXPAND ON IT

Here is another tool that you can use to make a decision. Think of a decision different from the one you just worked through that you are facing. List the pros and cons in the table. Next use the following five-point scale to rate each pro and con that you listed. This approach will help you determine the answer to your problem. The next time you have a decision to make, give the decisional-balancing activity a try. It may help you weigh up your options by looking at the costs and benefits. Often when you write down all of your options the answer will become clearer.

Pros	Score	Cons	Score

5 = Not important

4 = A little bit important

3 = Somewhat important

2 = Quite important

1 = Extremely important

THINK MINDFULLY

INTRODUCTION

Have you ever watched clouds float by in the sky? It's fun to watch clouds and make out their shapes. Sometimes clouds look like dragons, castles, dinosaurs, etc. After a while of watching the same cloud, it begins to lose its shape and dissipate. Did you know that thoughts are a lot like clouds? Here are some of their similarities:

- Some are big, some are small.

- They come in different shapes and sizes.

- Some are light and fluffy and some are scary and dark.

Yes, thoughts are very similar in that they come and go, change, and are often forgotten. In the same way that you cloud watch, you can learn thought watching. You can learn to let your thoughts come and go and float on by...

DIRECTIONS

Practice thoughtful meditation by engaging in the following activity, but before you get started you'll need a peaceful, comfy, and dark environment that's free from distraction. Set your phone alarm or a timer for five minutes. Get in a comfortable position lying on your back. Focus on listening to the sound of silence. Imagine looking at the sky and seeing clouds float by. For the next five minutes all you have to do is let your thoughts come and go like clouds, even if they are dark clouds. Let them float on by.

Did any of your thoughts linger longer than others? If so, write them down using a pencil. Just as a cloud breaks apart, so do thoughts. Take the troublesome thought and erase it; let it move away from you by releasing it. Some thoughts move slower than others. If you have a thought that won't move forward, acknowledge it and list what it is about this thought that is troubling to you. Next, identify small steps you can take to get the thought moving again. For example, you didn't make the basketball team or get the role you wanted in the school play, but does that make you a failure or is your thought making you feel like a failure? Not making a team or getting the role you want may be a disappointment, but it doesn't define who you are as a person. Only you hold the power to let your thoughts come and go. Watch them, acknowledge them, but don't hold onto them.

EXPAND ON IT

★ Try this...

Each time you have a thought that seems to be in slow motion, close your eyes and remind yourself that it's just a thought. Next start thinking about something pleasant, such as a recent family vacation or something that you are excited about doing. Visualizing pleasant memories, beautiful places, or thinking about exciting things are great distracters. Write down three healthy and pleasant distracters that you can focus on the next time that you have a slow moving thought.

1. _____
_____
_____
_____
_____

2. _____
_____
_____
_____
_____

3. _____
_____
_____
_____
_____

Chapter Four

ANXIETY AND EMOTIONS

Change involves self-reflection and that can be painful. It is where pain and discomfort exceed fear that change happens.

Chapter outline

Activity 4.1 Emotional Baggage

Activity 4.2 Stressed to the Max

Activity 4.3 Worrywart

Activity 4.4 Panic Free

Activity 4.5 Depression

Activity 4.6 Anger—The Cover-up

Activity 4.7 Facts before Feelings

Activity 4.8 Survival Raft

Chapter objectives

From this chapter you will:

- learn how carrying hurtful things around can increase anxiety
- learn about stress levels
- explore the power that fear and worry can have over you
- learn how to keep from panicking
- explore how depression and anxiety can go hand in hand
- explore the role of anger in anxiety
- learn to let go and stop fighting your demons.

Pre/post-scaling questions

Pre-question

This group of activities will help you gain a better understanding of how anxiety and your emotions go hand in hand. On a scale of 0 to 10, with zero being "no understanding" and 10 being "full understanding," rate your current level of understanding of how your level of anxiety affects your feelings. Plot the score on the grid below.

Post-question

This group of activities reviewed anxiety and your emotions. At the beginning of this chapter you rated yourself at a _____ (let them know the pre-score rating). Using the same scale of 0 to 10, with zero being "no understanding" and 10 being "full understanding," rate your current understanding of how your anxiety and feelings interact with one another. Plot the post-score on the grid below.

Here are some sample follow-up questions that can assist you in comparing and contrasting your clients scores:

- "I noticed that you moved from a '5' to a '6' on the scale. What are some things that contributed to you moving up?"

- "What are some things that you can do to help you move closer to a '10?'"

- "Are there any things that you feel you'd like to work on more in this chapter that would help you move up on the scale?"

- "I noticed that you didn't move up. Was there anything in particular that you wanted to explore in this section that we didn't cover?"

- "What are some things that can help you move up on the scale?"

- "What was the most helpful thing that you learned?"

- "What did you find not useful at all?"

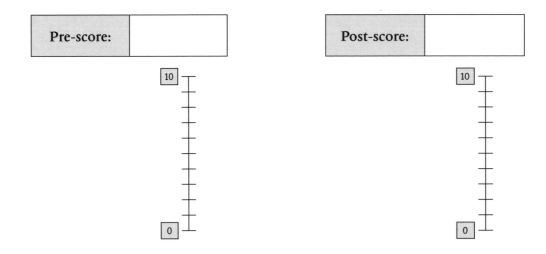

Activity 4.1

EMOTIONAL BAGGAGE

★

INTRODUCTION

Emotional baggage is holding onto the hurtful and unpleasant things of the past. This baggage can be a burdensome and heavy load to bear. It may also keep you from accomplishing things that you really want to. Did you know that carrying excess baggage is a choice? You have the power to choose to lighten your load or drag it with you in life.

Imagine...

You are carrying a really heavy suitcase on a very, very long journey. It's heavy and your feet are aching. You don't know if your back can take hauling this awkward luggage any longer. You have to stop frequently because the load is draining you emotionally and physically. In fact, because of its weight it is taking you longer to reach your destination. You are about ready to collapse. The road is long and winding and then one day you decide to open your luggage and see what's in it. You notice there are things that you are carrying that you really don't need. So, you decide to unpack your suitcase and take out items you don't need. You zip the suitcase back up leaving the excess items on the path. When you pick up the suitcase you realize how much lighter your load is; it's like a weight has been lifted off your shoulders.

Are you carrying a heavy load? If so, here are some do's and don'ts for emotional packing...

This is what you want to unpack in your emotional suitcase:

- Grudges against other people. It's time to let go of grudges and forgive. You may not forget, but forgiveness and forgetting are two separate things. It doesn't mean you'll be friends again or that you'll trust the person, it just means you are choosing to let it go and not let it haunt you any longer. Forgiveness will lighten your load.

- Your fears. Fears will keep you from trying new things. Many times fears are not rational and are based on something that may never happen. Try to keep your fears in perspective and don't carry them all through life.

- Regrets. A regret is something of the past. Take past mistakes and learn from them. If you regret not doing something then the next time something similar rolls around—do it. But don't waste your time and energy on something that you can't change now.

- Disappointments. Life is full of disappointments. Rather than focusing on past hurts, focus on what the future may hold. Disappointments are inevitable, but for every disappointment there are many more positives.

- Failures. You're not perfect and you are going to make mistakes. Failures can be turned into successes by learning from your mistakes. Don't stay focused on failures, rather learn from them and move in a forward motion.

This is what you want to pack in your emotional suitcase:

- Compliments others have given you.

★

- Positive memories that you cherish.

- Successes that you have had in life.

- Things that you are looking forward to.

- Good friendships and loving family members.

- The blessings bestowed on you daily. Don't get so absorbed in the negatives that you forget to pay equal attention to the positives.

So what are you waiting for? Start unpacking and reorganizing that luggage!

DIRECTIONS

Are you carrying a heavy load in your suitcase? You don't have to. Reorganize your baggage so it's not so heavy.

Suitcase one

In the suitcase, list all of the things that you carry with you each and every day; for example, negative memories, bad experiences, failures, hurtful things, disappointments, etc. Describe how this baggage makes you feel:

- emotionally

- mentally

- physically.

Unpack your heavy suitcase. List the things that you don't need to carry around any longer.

Suitcase two

Pack a bag of positives. If you focus on the positives you can pack as many of them as you want and they won't weigh you down. Describe how this new baggage makes you feel:

- emotionally

- mentally

- physically.

EXPAND ON IT

Get a balloon and small slips of paper. Write the hurtful things that you are holding onto on a slip of paper. Place each strip of paper that you write something on in the balloon. When you are finished, blow the balloon up, close your eyes, and focus on letting go of the baggage that is in your balloon. Open your eyes and release it all...

1. Let go of resentment.
2. Let go of embarrassment.
3. Let go of anger.
4. Let go of hurt.
5. Let go of fear.
6. Let go of guilt.
7. Let go of regret.
8. Let go of pain.
9. Let go of shame.
10. Let go of rejection.

List any others below...

Activity 4.2

STRESSED TO THE MAX

INTRODUCTION

Have you ever felt as if you just couldn't deal with one more thing that gets thrown at you? If one more thing gets added to your plate you're going to collapse. If so, join the millions of others who have fallen victim to being stressed to the max. Stress can be overwhelming. Plus stress distorts reality so that even small things seem humongous! Often some of the things we feel stressed about really aren't that big a deal, but because stress magnifies, even the smallest things seem bigger than they really are. You can deal with stress by realizing what's in your control to be stressed about and what's not. You don't have to be stressed to the max if you learn to control your levels of stress. Look at the top ten signs that you may be stressed. How many of them can you relate to?

Ten signs you may be stressed:

1. poor sleep

2. frequent headaches and/or gastrointestinal problems

3. anger outbursts

4. lack of concentration

5. increased levels of anxiety and/or panic episodes

6. overeating/undereating

7. increased sadness

8. social withdrawal

9. irritability

10. lack of motivation.

Look at what Darren does to help with his stress.

Darren was sitting in his counselor's office awaiting his session. "I really don't have time to be here," he thought. "I have so much to do!" He was called back into the office. "It's about time," Darren mumbled under his breath. His counselor of six months had picked up on his agitation. "Darren, you don't seem yourself today. Is there anything you want to discuss?" she asked. "I have too much to do and no time to do it!" Darren busted out. "I don't even have the time to be here," he added. "Sounds like you have a full plate and are overwhelmed. What if we could find a way to get some things off your plate?" his counselor asked. "If you can do that, it would be a miracle," Darren responded. "Well, then it's time we performed a miracle!" his counselor said lightheartedly.

"The name of what we are going to do, ironically, is called 'full plate', "his counselor said. Darren listened closely as his counselor helped him unravel all that he had going

126

on. First, the counselor took out a dinner plate and some sticky notes. She asked Darren to write each thing that he had going on in his life on a sticky note. Darren wrote down the following:

Karate: Wednesday and Thursday

Maths test: Friday

Study group: Thursday

Work: Monday, Tuesday, and Friday

Paper due: Friday

Grandparents are coming to visit for the next week

After Darren wrote everything down his counselor asked him to look at each thing he had on his plate and ask himself, "Is this something that I have control over?" Darren sorted through the sticky notes and put the ones he had control over in one pile and those he didn't into another pile. Darren was asked to put the things he had no control over to the side because there wasn't anything he could do about those and to focus on the pile he did have control over. The pile that was in his control he called the "Action pile" because Darren could come up with an action plan to work on those stressors. Here is what Darren came up with.

Action plan

Karate: Wednesday and Thursday—talk to instructor and only go on Wednesday. Add another day next week when the workload is less.

Maths test: Friday—study a little every day; don't wait until Thursday to tackle it.

Study group: Thursday—go to half of the study group and then leave to finish the paper.

Work: Monday, Tuesday, and Friday—switch off-days with another employee. I can work the weekend and usually it's an easy switch.

Paper due: Friday—work a little each day to get the paper done.

Grandparents coming to visit—no control—game plan: spend whatever time I can with them.

"Wow!" Darren said after the session, "I feel like a ton of weight has been lifted off me, thanks!" "I'm glad you feel better, Darren. Just remember that when your life feels as if it's falling apart, there are some things that you have control over. I will see you next session. Oh and Darren, remember not to put too much on your plate," his counselor said with a chuckle as she walked him out. "No, joke," Darren laughed back.

DIRECTIONS

 Have you ever felt like Darren? Having a full plate is stressful, but manageable, even if it doesn't feel like it. Give the full-plate exercise a try and write down all of the stressors in your life right now in the space below. Like Darren, develop a plan to focus on what needs to be handled. Circle the things that you do not have control over and move them off your plate for now. Next, look at the things you do have control over, this is your action plan. Now come up with an action plan for each stressor.

What's on your plate?

What's in your action pile?

What's your action plan?

EXPAND ON IT

In Darren's example he became agitated because he felt he had too much going on and couldn't handle it all. By looking at and addressing everything on his plate, he was able to stop looking on the inside out and look from the outside in. When you are caught in the middle of something it's hard to see the light at the end of the tunnel, but if you can separate yourself from the situation and look from the outside in, things may become clearer. Throughout life your plate will get full and you can use this technique to help you when life seems unbearable.

- Describe how stress makes you feel.

- Sort through your plate to help you cope better with life events.

Use this technique when you begin to feel stress coming on. You don't have to wait until you are stressed to the max to do something. In fact, by starting early you can head off a potential panic attack and feel in charge of your life at the same time.

WORRYWART

INTRODUCTION

Worrying is the feeling of being constantly anxious about something that is unpleasant that may have already happened or may happen. We have all experienced it and it is an uncomfortable feeling. If worrying preoccupies most of your day then you may just be a worrywart. By definition, a worrywart is someone who worries needlessly and excessively until it becomes habitual.

Did you know that you may be spinning your wheels worrying over things that you have no control over, or that may never happen? Now think about that for a second... Do you really have that much time to spend worrying your day away? People usually don't associate worrying with feeling good and happy. It is usually the opposite. Have you ever heard the saying "worried sick?" There is a reason for that saying. Worrying has been associated with physical illness, panic attacks, and even memory problems.

Desiree was a chronic worrier. Because of her excessive worrying she had earned the title "Worrywart." When she didn't have anything to worry about she would either find something or worry because she was afraid she was forgetting about something she should be worrying about. Her mind was constantly in a state of distress from all her worrying. One time Desiree had to face one of her big fears—flying all by herself. What should have been an exciting trip to visit her grandmother turned into a nightmare.

Rather than thinking about all of the fun stuff she was going to do her mind kept popping "what if" questions such as...

- *What if* I didn't pack everything?

- *What if* my ticket doesn't go through?

- *What if* airport security stops me because I didn't pack everything right?

- *What if* I miss my flight?

- *What if* I don't know how to get around the airport?

Needless to say everything turned out fine, as it usually did, but Desiree spent a good many sleepless nights with an upset stomach and sleep deprivation because she was worried. And once she got on the plane the next set of worries took their shift:

- *What if* I have to go to the bathroom before we are allowed?

- *What if* something happens to the plane?

- *What if* my grandparents forget to pick me up?

- *What if* the airport loses my baggage?

Desiree's anxiety kept her from enjoying what was supposed to be a fun vacation. She worried for the whole flight over something. And although she had a good time with her grandparents, she would have had a better stay if she hadn't worried so much.

After that trip Desiree decided to get a grip on her chronic worrying. It was like a bad habit that had to be broken. She decided to spend some time with the things that she worried about. She had spent too much time running from her worries so she set aside some time each day, not before bed or the worry would keep her up, and wrote down all of her worry thoughts including the dreaded *"what ifs."* She then rewrote them as *"so whats"* such as, "What if I forget to pack something? So what, I get to go shopping." Next, she looked at the worry that felt the most overwhelming: "What if my ticket doesn't go through?" To fix this worry she checked to make sure she had an electronic confirmation on her phone and she did. Then it was off to the next worry.

This new approach helped Desiree focus on only one thing at a time. At the end of the day she put her worries away and told them that they'd have their turn later. As humorous as this may sound, what she found is that each day she did this, the stuff that she had worried about the day before wasn't as big a deal. In the past, she would have let it beat her up and keep her from sleeping! If you are a worrywart you too can try Desiree's method. What do you have to lose? What might you have to gain?

DIRECTIONS

Without putting too much thought into it, jot down all the things you are worried about right now on the worrywart line. Below each thing you write, write down all of the "what ifs" attached to that worry. Last, counter them with "so whats."

Worrywart worry

"What ifs"

"So whats"

Worrywart worry

"What ifs"

"So whats"

Worrywart worry

"What ifs"

"So whats"

Worrywart worry

"What ifs"

"So whats"

Worrywart worry

"What ifs"

"So whats"

Worrywart worry

"What ifs"

"So whats"

Worrywart worry

"What ifs"

"So whats"

EXPAND ON IT

Set aside some time each day. Take a small notebook; this will be your worry journal. Each day around the same time, preferably not before bed, jot down every worry and the "what if" that is racing through your mind. Look at your list and circle one or two worries that need your immediate attention. Choose no more than two.

The remaining worries have to wait till tomorrow to have their turn to be addressed. Let them know they'll have another shot at it tomorrow. You don't have to worry about these right now because they don't need your immediate attention. You've already chosen your worry. Repeat this exercise daily. Soon you'll notice that many of the things you've been worrying about one day aren't even a worry the next.

PANIC FREE

INTRODUCTION

Panic is the feeling of being out of control. It's caused by high levels of anxiety. Panic attacks cause extreme physical sensations and no matter how scary they may seem, they usually are not harmful. Panic attacks are simply the activation of the stress response system called fight or flight. They are caused by the anticipation of a dreaded situation or future event. If they are persistent, they can hold you back in life.

Panic attacks are very real and very scary. People who experience them describe feelings of being out of control, feeling dizzy, having a hard time breathing, having a heart attack, and the list goes on and on... Everyone responds differently to a panic attack; take a look at Sarah Kate's experience:

> For the past year, Sarah Kate struggled with panic attacks. She had a lot of them during her maths class which was right after lunch. In fact, she rarely ate much at lunch because she had an extreme phobia of getting sick in class and throwing up. If the truth be known, that very thing had happened to her once in grade school when she caught a stomach bug in fifth grade. It was a humiliating experience and after that day she developed a fear that it would happen again. Over the years, the fear only got worse. When she got to high school her fear became uncontrollable.
>
> Each day after lunch Sarah Kate would go straight to class and sit in the desk closest to the door in case she needed to make a break for the bathroom. She spent most of her time focused on her fear rather than on class. As a result of her inability to concentrate she started to fail maths.
>
> She also lost a lot of weight in high school because her fear kept her from eating. She felt as if food was the culprit to her anxiety. Unfortunately, because she didn't eat much her stomach would often growl and make loud noises and that would make her feel as though everyone was watching her. Sarah Kate's thoughts became so intense and often when she was in the midst of a panic attack, she thought she was going to die. Her heart would race rampantly, her skin would get wet with sweat, she felt as if she had just sprinted a mile even though she was sitting at her desk, her stomach would cramp, and guess what? She thought she would throw up. Sarah Kate was becoming her own worst enemy. Panic raced through every vein of her body and she felt as if her world was crashing down. All of her panic was creating exhaustion and a feel of being drained.
>
> Fortunately, Sarah Kate made it through her high school years and is now studying psychology at college. Funny how life works out... After a lot of hard work and dedication, Sarah Kate is panic free. The secret to overcoming her panic attacks wasn't anything magical. In fact, it was simple, but took a lot of work and dedication—she followed five easy steps and conquered panic.

Step one—Identify situations that bring on panic. *Maths class.*

Step two—Identify your physical sensations. *Stomach ache and sweating.*

Step three—Identify feelings/emotions. Rate the emotion 1 to 10: 1 is the worst it's ever been and 10 is the best it's ever been.

- Where are you now? *2*
- Where do you need to be? *9*
- What will help you move up a point? *Eat a small snack and be calm in class.*
- How can you keep yourself at that point? *Take a snack into class and arrive before others to get settled.*

Step four—Identify toxic or unhelpful thoughts. *"Everyone thinks that I am weird."*

Step five—Do the BBRR (Break, Breathe, Relax, and Re-Group).

- Break—Take a break by getting out of the situation, if you can. Tell yourself *"time out."*
- Breathe—Take deep slow abdominal breaths and count to ten.
- Relax—Relax your muscles, body, and mind
- Re-Group—Re-group, if you have to face the situation do so with a fresh perspective.

If you put your efforts into these steps, they will help you live a life that is panic free.

DIRECTIONS

Like Sarah Kate, write out your own panic scenario. Follow through and complete the five steps to becoming panic free.

Step one—Identify situations that bring on panic.

Step two—Identify your physical sensations.

Step three—Identify feelings/emotions. Rate the emotion 1 to 10: 1 is the worst it's ever been and 10 is the best it's ever been.

- Where are you now?

- Where do you need to be?

- What will help you move up a point?

- How can you keep yourself at that point?

Step four—Identify toxic or unhelpful thoughts. Release them like releasing a helium balloon. They are just thoughts that have one goal: to keep you in panic mode.

Step five—Do the BBRR (Break, Breathe, Relax, and Re-group).

- Where will you go for a break?

- Practice abdominal breathing.

- Practice relaxation. Tense your body and release it slowly until you feel like a rag doll.

- Re-group—Write your scenario the way you would like it to end. Begin with the end in mind and work your way back to being panic-free.

EXPAND ON IT

Write the five on an index card, type them on your tablet or computer, or text them into your phone. If you experience a panic attack, practice the steps over and over again. In time they will become second nature. Be patient with yourself as you work to become panic free. The first week will be your most difficult.

Activity 4.5

DEPRESSION

INTRODUCTION

Depression can be described as feeling sad, blue, or unhappy. Most of us have felt depressed at some point in our lives. Usually these feelings come and go, but sometimes they linger for days and, worse still, months. When depressed feelings interrupt our lives and won't go away, then it's a signal that we need help.

Lizbeth battled with depression most of her life. Throughout middle school she suffered from severe panic attacks. She feared that one of her parents would get an incurable disease. She used to skip school to stay at home where she felt she would be closest to her parents if they needed her.

When she got to high school, her panic attacks began to go away, but she became controlling and had obsessive-compulsive tendencies. Lizbeth developed an acute fear of uncleanliness and a fear of contracting a disease because of germs. This really affected her life and her friendships as she would seek the comfort of her own home rather than going anywhere because she thought it would be filthy. She recalled not going to the bathroom during the school day and avoided drinking anything. Needless to say, she was miserable. Then she became extremely depressed.

Lizbeth remembered becoming extremely depressed, losing weight, and not sleeping. Thankfully, her worried parents sought medical help and she was diagnosed with an anxiety disorder and depression. With therapy and medication Lizbeth was able to get the help she needed. And now for once in her life, she is at peace and truly happy. Of course, not everyone needs the level of help that Lizbeth did, but the main thing to realize is you aren't condemned to feeling this way for the rest of your life. Peace and happiness await you; you just have to seek them.

DIRECTIONS

Answer "Yes" or "No" to each of the questions.

1. I am sad and unhappy more often than not.

2. I have pulled away from my friends and family.

3. I am moody more times than not.

4. I sleep a lot more than I used to.

5. I have trouble paying attention to things that are important.

6. I don't care about taking care of myself anymore.

7. I get agitated easily and I am angry most of the time.

8. I don't eat as much as I used to.

9. I don't like doing things that I once enjoyed doing.

10. I am lonely.

11. I don't have any friends.

12. I cry more than I used to.

13. I have lost weight.

14. I frequently get tired.

15. I frequently feel that I am worthless.

16. I don't have the same amount of energy that I used to.

17. People around me have noticed that I am unhappy.

18. I have difficulty falling asleep.

19. I fight a lot more with my family and friends.

20. I have recurrent thoughts of death and suicide.

21. I have thought about harming my body.

22. I have tried to harm my body.

23. I have lost pleasure and joy in my life.

24. I feel depressed.

25. I have difficulty making decisions.

26. I blame myself when things go wrong.

27. I frequently punish myself for something I do wrong.

28. I feel hopeless.

Check off each of the symptoms that you are currently experiencing.

- ❑ Indecisiveness
- ❑ Sadness
- ❑ Hopelessness
- ❑ Agitation
- ❑ Irritability
- ❑ Worthlessness
- ❑ Anger
- ❑ Periods of crying
- ❑ Fatigue
- ❑ No motivation

❑ Difficulty concentrating

❑ Restlessness

❑ Poor hygiene

❑ Sensitivity to disappointments/rejection

❑ Alcohol/drug use

❑ Significant weight changes (losing too much or gaining a lot)

❑ Risk-taking behaviors

❑ Self-harming behaviors

❑ Inability to focus

If you answered "yes" to questions 20–25 then please speak with your counselor immediately. Also if you answered "yes" more than "no" to any of the questions and checked off multiple symptoms you are indicating signs of depression. If you have depression you are not alone. People care about you and want to help. Please speak with your counselor about your symptoms.

EXPAND ON IT ←——→

If you scored high for depressive symptoms, which symptoms do you struggle with the most?

- How long have you been feeling this way?

- Have you spoken with someone about it? If so, who?

- What ways do you try to cope with feeling depressed?

- List some caring people in your life whom you can ask for help.

Millions of people have experienced depression. You are not alone. Just like anxiety, depression is treatable. You don't have to feel this way. There is help. Please reach out to a trusted adult and let him/her know how you are feeling.

Activity 4.6

ANGER—THE COVER-UP

INTRODUCTION

Anger is a normal emotion, but often it's a cover-up for another emotion. For example, stress, anxiety, hurt, shame, and depression have all been known to hide under the veil of anxiety. It's easier to be angry than to admit your feelings are hurt, or to be angry when you feel anxious about something that's coming up that you're dreading. Anger is a surface emotion that can keep you from going to the root of the problem. It takes a lot of time and energy to be angry, so you may get preoccupied with the anger and lose focus on what is underneath your anger. Unfortunately, when this happens the true issue or hurt doesn't heal, it just stays there and festers. Think of anger as a Band-Aid; it just covers a wound, but the wound is still there.

I'm Colton and I have been working on my anger issues for most of my life, but only recently it came to light that I had been tackling the wrong emotion all along. I started seeing a counselor and through therapy we discovered that the root of my angry outbursts was anxiety. Here's my story...

One day I misplaced my phone. I looked everywhere for it and couldn't find it. I got really stressed out because I knew if my parents found out I had lost it they would flip out, to say the least. The last time I had it was in the TV room and I tore that room apart looking for it. I became so anxious that my mind wouldn't let me get off the idea that that's where it was. I know you're probably thinking just call the phone yourself. Great idea, but the battery was dead, so that was out of the question.

I can't tell you how stressed I was. I begged my parents for that phone for my birthday, and even though they didn't think I was responsible enough, they went against their judgment and let me have it. I guess I wasn't responsible enough and I blew it. Then I started thinking that my brother probably messed with it. He came into the TV room when I was searching and I unleashed on him. I accused him of stealing it, tore up his room looking for it, and even slammed him into the wall a couple of times telling him that I'd hit him if he didn't turn it over. Even though he denied having it, I knew he was lying! I went to my room and punched a hole in the wall. Luckily it was a small hole, and I had got pretty good at plastering things, so I fixed it before anyone noticed. It had been two days since I had last seen my phone and I knew my parents would be asking anytime where it was.

One afternoon, when my mom got home for work, I noticed my phone was in her hands. "Missing something?" she asked. I smiled like I had just been caught red-handed. "Where did you find that?" I asked. "Under the seat where you left it when you went to karate the other night." "Oh yeah," I replied.

I tell my story only to show you how my stress and anxiety manifested in anger. I wasn't really angry at all, rather I was scared, stressed, and anxious. So, my therapist and I have been working to get to the root of what's bothering me and keep it from morphing into something it's not. We looked at how I was responding to anger through screaming, hitting, threatening, and damaging property. Clearly, these aren't ways to handle my anger and they sure didn't help me find my phone either. Then we did this trick called emotional separation.

Here's how it works when I get angry: I stop what I am doing and start writing down what I am really feeling and then I scale or rate the intensity of each emotion that I have listed. The one(s) with the highest score is what I have to work on controlling. Then I use realistic thinking to work my way backwards through the situation and try to control my anxiety.

So in my situation, anger was a reactionary emotion. Primary emotions were stress, fear, and anxiety. Fear rated the highest at a 10 because my parents would ground me for life if I lost that phone! So rather than going on a wild rampage, I revisited the situation, working on fear rather than anger. If I had retraced my steps and thought about where I had last seen my phone, I probably would have realized it was in my mom's car. Next time I lose something, I will stop what I am doing and take deep breaths. Then I'll retrace my steps and work backwards.

One thing that I learned from this experience is that anger clouds judgment. When you put your time and energy into what's really bothering you, you can get a lot more accomplished and feel more in control.

DIRECTIONS

What emotions are you guilty of concealing with anger?

1. As fast as you can, list all of the things that make you angry.

2. As fast as you can, list all of the ways that you respond to anger. For example, do you slam things around, destroy things, yell and scream, sulk, etc.?

3. Circle all of the emotions that you frequently feel. Add any that are not listed.

Affection	Doubt	Happiness	Pride
Amusement	Elation	Helplessness	Relief
Anger	Embarrassment	Hope	Sadness
Annoyance	Empathy	Hurt	Satisfaction
Anxiety	Envy	Interest	Shame
Boredom	Excitement	Irritation	Shock
Courage	Fear	Joy	Stress
Despair	Friendliness	Love	Trust
Disappointment	Frustration	Pleasure	Worry
Disgust	Guilt	Powerlessness	
_____	_____	_____	_____
_____	_____	_____	_____
_____	_____	_____	_____

4. Are most of the emotions that you circled positive or negative?

5. There are three Band-Aids below. In the center of each Band-Aid list the emotion that you cover with anger.

EXPAND ON IT

Complete the following statements:

- When I get angry I...

- I react to anger by...

- I use anger as a cover-up by...

- Coping with my real emotions rather than anger will help me...

- The next time that I get angry, I will identify what I am really feeling and...

Activity 4.7

FACTS BEFORE FEELINGS

★

INTRODUCTION

Often when people are stressed or feel overwhelmed they put their feelings before the facts. When this happens things can get messy.

Jacob was having a hard time focusing in class. He had just received his score back on a project he had worked really hard on. When he turned it in, he had felt confident that he aced it, but when he got his grade he ended up getting a low score. A lot of his friends did well on the project, but Jacob knew that he had spent more time on his than they had on theirs. He was embarrassed by the low grade and he immediately wanted to drop the course.

Jacob went to speak with his school counselor about dropping the course. Jacob got choked up as he told the counselor about his poor grade. She sat back and listened to his story unfold. By the time he had finished telling her everything, she looked at him and said, "Jacob, it sounds as if you have your feelings before your facts. You are saying you want to drop the course because you feel bad about the grade you received. You don't feel as if you will make a good grade in the class because of one low grade. You feel the teacher has it in for you and is treating you unfairly. But what about the facts? What about the fact you have a good grade in the class already? What about the fact that this was only one bad grade? You see, when your feelings get ahead of your facts, you can get sidetracked and lose control of a situation. You may make irrational decisions based only on your feelings because you're ignoring the facts."

After speaking with his counselor Jacob felt more in control of the situation and saw how his feelings led him away from the facts. Jacob left his counselor with the reminder to put facts before feelings and then draw conclusions based on the facts. He went back to class and made an appointment to speak with his teacher so he could gain a better understanding of the poor score he had got. He was determined to do better on the next assignment.

DIRECTIONS

Look at each of the scenarios below and write whether the statement is a fact or feeling statement.

1. Everything sucks.

2. I am having a bad day.

3. I hate this class.

4. The teacher assigns two hours of homework every night.

5. I can't do this; it's too hard.

6. There is a lot to memorize for the test.

7. I'm a failure.

8. I got a poor grade on the test.

9. I'll freak out.

10. I am nervous.

11. No one likes me.

12. We are having a disagreement.

13. You can never trust anyone.

14. He betrayed my trust.

15. I will never be able to show my face again.

16. I am embarrassed.

17. I am not going to get through this.

18. I am overwhelmed.

19. I always screw everything up.

20. I made a mistake.

How to score your responses: All odd number responses are feeling responses. All even number responses are facts.

Were you able to sort the facts from the feelings? Sometimes it's good to have some personal facts about yourself already picked out so when the feelings hop before the facts, you'll be able to switch them back into the proper order. For example, what are some personal facts about you? Are you witty, funny, likable, caring, compassionate, artistically or musically talented, or athletic? We all have facts about our personality. In the space provided write facts about yourself. Use these the next time your feelings pull ahead of the facts.

EXPAND ON IT

Do you get your feelings before your facts? Think of a recent situation in which you did not act appropriately. Describe the situation below:

In each column write the facts and feelings:

Facts	Feelings

Refer back to your list and answer the following questions:

- Which drove your actions: facts or feelings? Odds are, if you reacted poorly, feelings were in the driver's seat.

- Describe why it's not a good idea to let feelings drive your behavior.

- Describe why it's good to let facts drive your behavior.

★

SURVIVAL RAFT

INTRODUCTION

Difficult thoughts and feelings interfere with your behaviors and ultimately your goals. When you listen to negative voices you may feel insecure and shy away from what you really want to do in life, giving those voices the power to control you. To examine this issue in more depth, look at this example of a survival raft.

The passengers on the raft

Imagine that you are in a very large raft and are navigating your way down a beautiful, yet challenging river. Pretend this raft represents your journey in life. It's heading in the direction of your values. For example, if you value being a kind person or being a hardworking student, that's the direction you're guiding your raft. Earlier you used a value compass to help you determine and clarify the direction in which your life was heading and are steering your raft in that direction.

Along the way you pick up passengers. Many of the passengers are nice and pleasant and you enjoy their company. Some are indifferent and don't really cause any problems. And then there are those passengers who try to tip the boat, steer you off course, and make you get stuck in an area where you don't want to be. At first you may try to keep them off your raft, but they won't move! These passengers are annoying and cause a lot of pain and hurt. They are loud, aggressive, ugly, nasty, and obnoxious. They tell you that you can't row your boat, that you are a failure, and that you are going the wrong way. They bully you and cause you to feel insecure.

Now, remember you are the guide of this boat, so you have power over the situation. You can definitely put these passengers off your boat or throw them overboard. However, if your passengers represent something that you've struggled with your whole life, they'll just keep popping up at different points of time on your journey. They will try to put sticks, rocks, and other obstacles in your way to make your journey more difficult. They may even try to steer you towards a waterfall! If you fight them long enough, eventually they will win.

Fortunately, there is another option: let them on and don't fight with them. Let them know you're the guide and you're in charge. Set the rules and send them to the back of the raft. Who knows, they may get bored and choose to hop off? If you keep on course with your eyes on your compass you'll find yourself enjoying the scenery of the journey. If you constantly fight your annoying passengers, you'll miss out on what life has to offer!

DIRECTIONS

Imagine you are guiding your life boat.

Write down your values in life. Remember, values are important and meaningful to you.

Write down what you could do to make this value more apparent in your life.

List some goals that you can set that will take you toward your values. These will be your stops along the way.

Describe the passengers on your raft in relation to your anxiety.

- Who are the kind passengers?

- Who are the most annoying?

- Who are the most hurtful?

EXPAND ON IT

Examine your list. Think about your life and the decisions you have made to try to put up with these passengers. Write down the following:

- How long have you fought them?

- How long will you allow them to take you off course?

- Describe the changes you are willing to make in your life to gain control of your survival raft.

Rather than fighting with non-cooperative passengers, would you consider staying on course with your values and letting them tag along, as long as they follow the rules you set? Keep your eyes on your destination and let your personal nuisances remain in the back of the boat. *Bon voyage!*

Chapter Five

ANXIETY AND BEHAVIOR

Anxiety is changeable. Below are the formulas for change. Which one will you choose?

Anxiety-driven life

Negative thoughts + feel-bad emotions = negative behaviors/actions

Anxiety-free life

Positive thoughts + feel-good emotions = positive behaviors/actions

Chapter Outline

Activity 5.1 Behavioral Checklist

Activity 5.2 Internalizing—Positives and Negatives

Activity 5.3 Externalizing Behaviors

Activity 5.4 Fears and Phobias

Activity 5.5 Perfectly Imperfect

Activity 5.6 Obsessions and Compulsions

Activity 5.7 Stress: Friend or Foe?

Activity 5.8 Outside Looking In

Activity 5.9 Meditation

Chapter objectives

From this chapter you will:

- learn to let go of hurtful things
- explore things that you fear
- explore things that you obsess over
- learn to view stress as a friend rather than an enemy
- explore your life from an outsider's perspective.

Pre/post-scaling questions

Pre-question

In this chapter you will explore the relationship between your anxiety and your behavior. On a scale of 0 to 10, with zero being "none at all" and 10 being "a lot," rate how much you think your anxiety affects your behavior. Plot the score on the grid below.

Post-question

This chapter explored your anxiety and your behavior. At the beginning of this chapter you rated yourself at a _____ (let them know the pre-score rating). Using the same scale of 0 to 10, with zero being "none at all" and 10 being "a lot," rate your current understanding of how your anxiety and behavior interact with one another. Plot the post-score on the grid below.

Here are some sample follow-up questions that can assist you in comparing and contrasting your client's scores:

- "I noticed that you moved from an '8' to a '10' on the scale. What are some things that contributed to you moving up?"

- "Are there any things that you feel you'd like to work on more in this chapter that would help you move up on the scale?"

- "I noticed that you didn't move up. Was there anything in particular that you wanted to explore in this section that we didn't cover?"

- "What are some things that can help you move up on the scale?"

- "What was the most helpful thing that you learned?"

- "What did you find not useful at all?"

- "Describe how anxiety keeps you from being the person that you want to be."

- "Describe the person that you want to be."

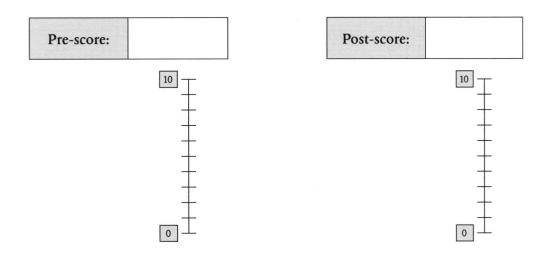

BEHAVIORAL CHECKLIST

INTRODUCTION

For the most part your behaviors are under your control, but anxiety can make it extremely hard to control bad habits and desires. There are many negative habits and behaviors that are associated with anxiety and stress. Some people may experience a few, while others experience many. The behaviors may also vary in intensity. It's important to understand how your anxiety is affecting you, and identifying your anxious behaviors is a good way to start.

DIRECTIONS

Learn more about which behaviors are related to anxiety by completing the behavioral checklist.

What you've been told...

Answer "yes" or "no" to the following questions:

Have you been told more times than not...

1. "You're too hard on yourself."
2. "Stop internalizing everything."
3. "It's not your fault."
4. "You put too much pressure on yourself."
5. "No one is perfect."
6. "You worry too much."
7. "You can't please everyone."
8. "You can't make everyone like you."
9. "Just because one person said it, doesn't mean it's true."
10. "Don't take everything so personally."

Tally your answers:

Number of "yes" responses: _____ Number of "no" responses: _____

Anxious symptoms

Answer "yes" or "no" to the following questions:

Have you ever had any of these anxious symptoms?

1. Stomach problems: diarrhea, stomach cramps, nausea, digestive problems?
2. Headaches?
3. Muscle aches?
4. Acne breakouts or other skin conditions such as hives or rashes?
5. Shortness of breath?
6. Dizziness?
7. Hot or cold flashes?
8. Erratic heartbeats?
9. Dry mouth or difficulty swallowing?
10. Chest pain?

List any other symptom that you get when you are anxious. Count each symptom that you write as a "yes" response.

Tally your answers:

Number of "yes" responses: _____ Number of "no" responses: _____

Behavioral characteristics

Write "yes" or "no" to any of the characteristics below that describe you:

1. Agitated
2. Anxious
3. Depressed
4. Destructive
5. Edgy
6. Fearful
7. Fretful
8. Impatient
9. Impulsive
10. Inattentive
11. Jumpy

★

12. Lonely

13. Nervous

14. Paranoid

15. Restless

16. Sad

17. Scared

18. Shy

19. Skittish

20. Suspicious

21. Withdrawn

22. Worried

List any other characteristic that describes you; count each characteristic that you write as a "yes" response.

Tally your answers:

Number of "yes" responses: _____ Number of "no" responses: _____

Habitual behaviors

Write "yes" or "no" to any of the habitual behaviors below that you experience:

1. Eating too much

2. Excessive tweezing

3. Eye twitching

4. Hair pulling

5. Jaw popping

6. Knuckle popping

7. Leg twitching

8. Nail biting

9. Not eating enough

10. Scab picking

11. Skin picking

12. Sleep problems

13. Stuttering

14. Teeth grinding

15. Temper tantrums

List any other habitual behavior that you engage in; count each habit that you write as a "yes" response.

Tally your answers:

Number of "yes" responses: _____ Number of "no" responses: _____

Things you do

Write "yes" or "no" to any of the things you do below that you most often experience.

1. Avoiding situations that make you uncomfortable

2. Being depressed

3. Being shy

4. Displaying aggression towards others

5. Drinking too much

6. Harming yourself

7. Having anger outburst

8. Having sex

9. Lying

10. Procrastinating

11. Skipping school

12. Stealing

13. Swearing

14. Taking drugs

15. Vandalizing things

List any other external behavior in which you engage; count each external behavior that you write as a "yes" response.

Tally your answers:

Number of "yes" responses: _____ Number of "no" responses: _____

Tally your total answers:

Number of total "yes" responses: _____ Number of total "no" responses: _____

How is anxiety affecting you? What did your score reveal?

Write down your first thoughts about your results on the behavioral checklist.

EXPAND ON IT

Look for patterns in your responses. Beside each response you listed write what you would need to happen to stop that behavior.

Answer the questions:

1. In each category on the checklist write the most troublesome behavior in which you engage and how long you have been doing it.

   What you've been told...

   Anxious symptoms

   Behavioral characteristics

   Habitual behaviors

   Things you do

2. Did any patterns emerge in responses to the behavioral checklist? If so, explain.

3. Describe some proactive things that you can do to help you with the troublesome behaviors.

Activity 5.2

INTERNALIZING—POSITIVES AND NEGATIVES

★

INTRODUCTION

Internalizing anxiety is holding all your feelings in and bottling them up. While this may work in the short term, its effects won't last long. Eventually, the stuff that you're stuffing can't be contained anymore and will spew out. When this happens you might as well call in the hazardous materials team because it's usually not good. Anxious people are notorious for bottling up emotions. If these feelings are not dealt with they can have adverse effects on your physical health, mental health, and your social life.

Victoria thought back to her high school years and remembered more positive than negative experiences. She also remembered more bad than good things said about her. She was like a sponge that soaked up everything. Victoria remembered being called names like "ugly," "fat," and "stupid." After a while she began to believe the hurtful words. One day, her sister asked her why she constantly played negative things over and over again in her head. "It's like all you ever think about are the negative things. You should try focusing on some positives too, Victoria; it would probably make you feel better."

Victoria thought about what her sister had said, but the truth was that she didn't know why she focused more on the unhealthy thoughts rather than the healthy ones... These things were said years ago and she still held onto them as if they were some universal truth. In fact, there was nothing wrong with her. She was smart and beautiful. Her sister's comment made her think about the things she was telling herself over and over again.

From that day forward, Victoria decided to soak up positives surrounding her and not negatives. There were times when hurtful thoughts would try to invade her mind, but she would quickly tuck them away and not let them take the spotlight off the positives. Although it took some time to learn how to stop internalizing beliefs, Victoria was able to take scars from the past and heal them. Here are some things that she learned through the process:

- Stop holding onto pain. Ask yourself—how is playing unhealthy thoughts over and over again in my head helping me?

- Don't blame yourself for other people's problems. It's not your fault.

- Forgive and let go. The first step in getting better is forgiving yourself and others. Start with a clean slate. Forgiving doesn't mean forgetting, it just means you don't have to hold onto it. Once you forgive, let it go—all the way. Don't carry it with you anymore.

- Surround yourself with friends and family. We need supports in our life. It's essential for survival. We wouldn't be in this world if it were only us. People are put on this earth to

153

love and help each other. So stop isolating yourself and get out there; get your support system together.

- Not everyone is going to like you and you're not going to make everyone happy all the time; it's a fact of life. You aren't perfect and you are not alone. No one is perfect: say that out loud until you believe it.

- Life is not all about competition. You don't have to compare yourself to others. Accept the person in the mirror. Celebrate your individuality; no one is like you.

- Live in the present. Don't look back; there's nothing you can do about the past. Today is all that matters, because today is all you have. Go ahead and enjoy it. Don't worry about the future, because it's not here yet. Plus, what you worry about may never even happen and then you've spent a whole lot of time worrying over nothing. Life's a mystery, so stop trying to figure it out.

- Draw your energy from positives, not negatives. Negative energy will zap and drain you. Positive energy will energize and uplift you. Look for the positive forces in life and recharge that battery before you become depleted.

DIRECTIONS

On average, do you soak up more negative comments and experiences than positive ones? Look at the example below and write the negatives that you're holding onto. Work through them and then follow the eight steps above to let them go.

Example:

Comment or thought: "You're ugly."

Reaction: This person thinks I'm ugly.

Internalizing reaction: I am ugly. Everyone thinks that I am ugly. If someone says that I am pretty or cute, he/she must be lying.

Redirecting: One person said that I am ugly. That was unkind. He/she must be having a bad day or he/she is unkind. I am not ugly.

Your turn. Write negative comments or things that you're holding onto.

1. Comment or thought:

Reaction:

Internalizing reaction:

Redirecting:

2. Comment or thought:

Reaction:

Internalizing reaction:

Redirecting:

3. Comment or thought:

Reaction:

Internalizing reaction:

Redirecting:

Don't let unhealthy thoughts weigh you down. The next time you find yourself focusing on unhealthy thoughts use one of the eight steps to redirect your thoughts back to something more healthy.

EXPAND ON IT

Focusing on the positives and negatives

Draw two circles. Label one "Positive" and the other "Negative." Write down as many negative things that you have internalized from your past that you can think of. These can be hurtful events, names that you have been called, bad choices that you have made, etc. In the positive circle, record all of the wonderful things that have happened. These can be positive memories, compliments, awards, accomplishments, etc.

Close your eyes and focus on the negative circle. Open your eyes and in the space below record how all those negative forces feel.

★

Close your eyes and focus on the positive circle. Open your eyes and in the space below describe how all those positive forces feel.

Notice how the negative circle feels as if it depletes you while the other is the circle of life filled with hope, optimism, and happiness.

Describe the circle you want to stand out the most in your life.

List five things you can do in the next week to surround yourself with positive forces. Make a plan to do these things and then write in the space below how you felt after you did them. You don't have to stop after you do this activity; keep it going! Live life to the fullest, and bask in the positives that it brings.

Activity 5.3
EXTERNALIZING BEHAVIORS

INTRODUCTION

Some people take all of their emotions and push them outward. Bottled emotions can come out in the form of hitting, swearing, screaming, threatening, throwing a fit, and hurting yourself. You can only hold in so much stuff before you blow up. This outward display of emotion is called *externalizing behaviors*.

Imagine a full fizzy drink bottle. What happens if you shake it and then open it? If you said explode or spew, good job. That's exactly what externalizing behavior is. It's the explosion and release of all the bottled-up junk in your life. So how do you get rid of it? The answer may be easier than you think. You find healthy ways to release what you are feeling and then you slowly release it. Think back to that fizzy drink bottle; if you shake it really hard, and slowly release the pressure it will not explode. Rather, by slowly releasing the pressure, you will see the bubbles rise to the top, and you can close it before they come out and then slowly open it again. Repeat this until all the pressure is released and then open the bottle. No mess! The secret—don't keep things bottled up.

DIRECTIONS

1. Inside your bottle write all of the stuff that you are currently bottling up. For example, are you stressed because your parents are fighting, you and your girlfriend/boyfriend broke up, you failed a big test, you didn't make the school team, you didn't get a part in the play, or your boss cut your hours at work?

2. Beside each item you listed rank it on a stress scale. For example, a 1 would mean that it doesn't bother you at all, whereas a 5 would mean it drives you insane!

   a. How many high raters do you have?

   b. What's your biggest stressor(s)?

   c. How long have you been bottling each item up?

   d. How full is your bottle?

3. Describe what happens when you explode. What emotions come out? How do you feel right after it happens? For example, does it feel good to get it all out or do you regret how you reacted?

4. List five or more things that help you release some of the steam that you're holding in. For example, go for a walk, talk to someone about what you're holding in, throw some darts at the dartboard, kick a heavy bag, draw a picture, bake a cake, go for a bike ride, etc.

   a. What is your favorite way to release pressure?

   b. How often do you do it?

   c. What keeps you from doing it more often?

   d. How can having outlets prevent an explosion?

EXPAND ON IT

Create and decorate your own emotional deposit bottle. When you feel that you are holding something in and it's beginning to build and fester, write it on a slip of paper and deposit it in your bottle. Next, look at one of your release activities and do it. For each deposit do a release. Don't worry if your bottle gets full, either empty it or toss it and start a new one. Metaphorically, we all carry a bottle with us in life; the key is to keep it from getting full and exploding.

FEARS AND PHOBIAS

★

INTRODUCTION

Whether it's spiders, new places, heights, or crowds, we all fear something in life. We may try to avoid the things that make us uncomfortable, but usually most people learn to manage and cope with their fear and go about their daily life. Unfortunately, there are some who can't overcome it and it becomes so intense that it keeps them from doing anything associated with their fear, even if there's no real threat.

This type of intense fear is called a *phobia*. Phobias are excessive and irrational fears which leave their victim feeling powerless and in anticipation that something bad is going to happen, even though the odds of it happening are slim to none. The sad thing about phobias is that they can paralyze and keep a person from trying new things or even enjoying life. But it doesn't have to be that way. By facing the very things you are afraid of you can overcome your fears and phobias.

Exposure therapy is one way to face your fears. In exposure therapy you learn to confront and face what you fear. The premise behind this approach is that the more you're exposed to the fear, the less likely you are to be afraid. You can practice exposure by climbing a ladder which is a step-by-step plan to confront the things you fear. Look at the example below.

Michael had an extreme fear of dogs. He would avoid them and would freak out if one came near him. When he was young it was more acceptable for him to be afraid, but now that he was older, he felt silly freaking out when a large dog came close to him. So, with the help of a counselor, Michael decided to overcome his fear of dogs through exposure exercises. He created a step-by-step plan to slowly confront his fear. Here is Michael's plan:

Step one—Identify the fear.

Dogs.

Step two—List your beliefs about your fear.

1. Dogs bite and I will get bitten.

2. Dogs are unpredictable and can attack me.

3. Dogs are unclean and their slobber has germs.

4. Dogs are ferocious.

5. Dogs can kill.

These are a few of the thoughts that haunted Michael.

Step three—Acknowledge how you feel, think, and act when you're around the thing you fear.

I feel...unsettled, scared, like something bad will happen.

I think...run before it attacks you! Get away fast before I get bitten!

I act...all jittery. If a dog comes close to me I scream and bolt. I've even hopped on a table in a crowded room before when a dog came in. Boy, did that cause a scene!

Step four—Do a reality check

Reality—I have never been hurt by a dog. It's just my thoughts getting ahead of me and fearing the "what ifs" rather than staying focused on what's really happening.

Step five—Climbing the Fear Ladder

State your goal: to pet a dog without freaking out.
Next, with the help of the counselor, Michael wrote out a plan to help him achieve his goal. They used small steps to help him lead up to petting a dog.

Step-by-step plan...

1. Look up pictures of dogs on the internet.
2. Read books about dogs.
3. Watch some shows on TV about dogs.
4. Stand at a distance and watch as people walk their dogs.
5. Make an appointment with a dog rescue charity and have a worker take me through the facility.
6. Arrange a way to meet and pet a friend's dog.

Michael slowly worked through all the steps. Once he conquered his fear he felt great. He learned that he could face his fears. While it was going to take Michael a while to overcome his fear of dogs completely, he was making slow and steady progress. It was a big accomplishment not to freak out every time a dog came near him. Maybe one day in the near future, he'll be able actually to pet one!

DIRECTIONS

Overcome your own fears in life one step at a time by designing your own exposure plan and creating a step-by-step plan to confront it.

Step one—Identify your fear.
List a fear or phobia that you would like to overcome.

Step two—Describe why you're afraid.
What thoughts swim through your head about your fear?

Step three—Acknowledge how you *feel, think, and act* when you are around the thing you fear.

I feel...

I think...

I act...

Step four—Do a reality check
Confront your fears. Are they rational? How likely is it that your fears happen in real life?

Step five—Climbing the Fear Ladder
Walk through each step to overcome your fear.

State your goal:

List a step-by-step process to confront your fear. Start small and lead up to your goal.

1.
2.
3.
4.
5.
6.

EXPAND ON IT

Once you achieve your goal, use the space below to write about it. Describe how it felt to overcome your fear. Did you think you could ever do it? Was it as bad as you thought? Do you think you could do it again?

Overcoming fear is hard, but it's not impossible. You are stronger than you think you are! Take time to acknowledge and celebrate each step you achieve because you deserve it and you're accomplishing what you set out to achieve!

Activity 5.5

PERFECTLY IMPERFECT

INTRODUCTION

What is perfect? Does such a thing exist? For a perfectionist "perfect" consists of living without error or mistake. In the real world, perfect is only a figment of the imagination. It is a fictional concept which brings stress and anxiety to those who hold it to be true.

If you're a perfectionist, somewhere along life's path you've drawn the erroneous conclusion that your best isn't good enough. You've bought into the concept that your mistakes corrupt you and that has led to disappointment. There is a difference between giving something your all and striving for perfection. Did you know that you will grow and learn the most from your mistakes? It's true. You are not a failure, you are not the sum of your mistakes, and you are perfectly imperfect!

DIRECTIONS

Are you a perfectionist? Take the quiz below to see by answering "yes" or "no" to each statement.

1. Do you often feel that your best isn't good enough?

2. Do you frequently start over when you mess up on something?

3. Do you often get stressed out or anxious when you screw up?

4. Do you look for more wrongs than rights in things that you do?

5. Do you often beat yourself up over mistakes?

6. Do you frequently play things you did wrong over and over again in your mind?

7. Do you worry more often than not about failing or not succeeding at a task?

8. Do you become stressed when you hand in an assignment because you think you could have done more?

9. Do you get anxious or stressed when someone is better at something than you are and then push yourself to work harder?

10. Do you put undue stress on yourself to achieve?

11. Do you continuously tell yourself that the secret to success is just to work harder?

12. Do you feel as if you're constantly in competition with others?

13. Do you often feel that others have also to perform up to your standards?

14. Do you avoid asking for help because you feel it's a sign of weakness?

15. Do you place extremely high expectations on yourself?

Scoring: Each statement is a characteristic of perfectionism. How many did you answer "yes" to? The more "yeses" that you have, the more perfectionist characteristics you possess. Explore why you put stress on yourself to be perfect by answering the questions below.

1. On a scale of 1–10, with 1 being the minimum and 10 being the maximum, rate the level of anxiety that your perfectionist characteristics cause in your life.

2. Have you ever worked really hard at something and not succeeded? Describe what happened.

3. How did you cope with your disappointment?

4. What did you learn from the failure?

EXPAND ON IT

Failure and mistakes are a part of life. Look at the quotes below about making mistakes and write a statement about their meaning.

Success is to be measured not so much by the position that one has reached in life as by the obstacles which he has overcome.

Booker T. Washington, Up from Slavery (*1901*)

I don't measure a man's success by how high he climbs but how high he bounces when he hits bottom.

George S. Patton

Success is a lousy teacher. It seduces smart people into thinking they can't lose.

Bill Gates, The Road Ahead *(1996)*

Never give in. Never give in, never, never, never, never—in nothing, great or small, large or petty—never give in, except to convictions of honour and good sense. Never yield to force: never yield to the apparently overwhelming might of the enemy.

Winston Churchill, Speech to boys at Harrow School (29 October 1941)

Veni, vidi, vici.

I came, I saw, I conquered.

Julius Caesar, Inscription in Caesar's Pontic triumph

Difficulties are just things to overcome after all.

Ernest Shackleton, The Heart of the Antarctic *(1909)*

All of these people made tremendous contributions to their field because of their imperfections. Their mistakes helped shape them into who they became. Your imperfection makes you perfect! Accept it and celebrate it.

Activity 5.6

OBSESSIONS AND COMPULSIONS

★

INTRODUCTION

It's normal to go back occasionally and double-check that you unplugged something or see that your car is locked. But if you have Obsessive Compulsive Disorder (OCD), obsessive thoughts and compulsive behaviors are in excess and interfere with your everyday life. OCD is an anxiety condition that involves persistent and unwanted thoughts which occur repeatedly followed by a ritualistic behavior. Although people with OCD may realize that their thoughts and actions are irrational, they cannot seem to stop them.

Obsessions

Obsessions are persistent thoughts, images, or impulses that occur repeatedly, making the person feel out of control. Key concepts about an obsession:

- The person feels the obsessions are outside his/her control.

- The person does not want to have the reoccurring thoughts and feelings.

- The thoughts are uncomfortable feelings such as fear, disgust, uncertainty, or a feeling that things have to be done to perfection.

- The obsessions interfere with the person's everyday functioning.

(*DSM-5* 2013)

Common obsessions

- Cleanliness—fear of germs, dirt, environmental pollutants, and/or body fluids.

- Unwelcome sexual thoughts—sexual thoughts about others, and/or obsessions with sexuality.

- Harm—fear of hurting or harming another person.

- Forgetting—fear that you will forget to turn off an appliance or lock a door, or turn on your alarm clock, which leads to constant checking.

- Losing control—fear of acting on violent or sexual ideas. This person struggles to suppress these urges and fears losing control.

- Perfectionism—an intense feeling that everything has to be perfect or just right. Undue stress is placed on having things orderly and done without flaw.

(*DSM-5* 2013)

Compulsions

Compulsions are the repetitive actions that a person does to reduce anxiety. Compulsions are often tied to an obsession and the compulsion is a way to alleviate the obsession. For example, if a person has an obsession with cleanliness and fears germs (obsession with germs) he/she may try to become more clean by repeatedly washing his/her hands (compulsion). Key concepts about a compulsion:

- Compulsions are repetitive behaviors or thoughts that a person has to try to control the obsession.

- Person understands this is a broken way to fix the problem, but doesn't have another solution.

- Compulsions can also include avoidance of uncomfortable situations.

- Compulsions are time consuming and interfere with the person's daily life.

(*DSM-5* 2013)

Common compulsions

- Hand washing or constantly cleaning to feel that things are clean and orderly.

- Checking things to make sure they are turned off, locked, or that a mistake wasn't made.

- Repetition by performing routine activities, excessive rereading or rewriting to make sure it's right.

- Habitual skin picking or finger nail biting.

- Counting while doing a task so it can end on a "safe" number.

- Hoarding items so that they cause extreme clutter.

- Placing things in an orderly fashion so that everything is perfect.

- Avoiding situations that cause obsessions.

(*DSM-5* 2013)

If you have OCD, or even if you just struggle with an obsession or compulsion, there are some things that you can do to work through the behavior. First, expose yourself to the very thing you're obsessing about and then keep yourself from performing the compulsive behavior in which you usually engage. For example, if you are a compulsive hand washer, touch something you think is dirty and then don't allow yourself to wash your hands. As you wait to wash, your anxiety will eventually begin to subside without you feeling the need to take care of it immediately. Over time you will learn that you don't need to do the compulsive behavior to get rid of anxiety, and that you can control it on your own. Plus, you can use positive self-talk to work your way through the obsessive situation.

Tyler struggled with OCD. He had an extreme obsession with germs in public bathrooms. In fact, he refused to go to any restroom in public because he feared that he would contract an incurable disease, not to mention he was embarrassed to be in public with his hand-washing ritual which took at least ten minutes. He feared others would talk about how weird he was if they knew... The majority of the time, Tyler could work around his need to go to the bathroom, but when at school he had to alter his whole life to avoid having to go. He would avoid eating or drinking anything and if an urge hit he would hold it to the point of being physically uncomfortable.

One day Tyler had had enough. He approached his parents and therapist about ways to overcome his fear of public restrooms. Together they came up with a game plan.

The next day Tyler and his parents went to visit the school counselor, Ms. Logan. She was already aware of Tyler's condition, but didn't realize how much it was affecting his functioning at school. Together they brainstormed a way for Tyler to start going to a public restroom at school. Ms. Logan mentioned that Tyler could use the faculty restroom near her office. She said that not many people used it, only teachers and staff, and they were a lot neater than the students. Although the first week was nerve-wracking, Tyler started going to a public restroom without freaking out!

Now Tyler can go to the restroom when he needs to because he confronted his OCD and realized that the only thing that was holding him back in the past was himself. One thing Tyler learned from this experience was that no matter what you're struggling with... if you want to change it you can. You just have to believe that you can.

DIRECTIONS

1. List your obsessions. Describe how they interfere with your life.

2. List your compulsions. Describe how they interfere with your life.

3. Describe what you would like to do that your OCD keeps you from doing.

4. Design a plan to expose yourself to your obsession and to react differently to the compulsion.

5. Describe what you will expose yourself to:

6. Rather than resorting to your compulsion, describe how you will confront it:

7. List some positive words or phrases that you will say to yourself as you are working through the situation. You may want to write these on a separate piece of paper to have with you, or record them to play back as you are working through the situation.

EXPAND ON IT

Keep practicing exposure and different reactions to your obsessions and compulsions. Odds are you didn't develop your OCD overnight, so it's going to take time to confront and successfully overcome it. The more you succeed, the more in control you will feel.

STRESS: FRIEND OR FOE?

INTRODUCTION

Is stress your friend or foe (enemy)? Most people would say enemy. It's bad for your health; it can lead to heart problems, high blood pressure, high cortisol levels, and even obesity. What's good about that? In addition, stress keeps you awake at night, makes you anxious, and immobilizes you so you can't do things. With a friend like that, who needs an enemy?

But *what if...what if* stress wasn't really all that bad? Do you know that studies have shown that stress isn't a big problem to your health, or your life for that matter? The problem lies in whether you perceive stress as a friend or a foe. As an enemy, stress can wreak complete havoc on your life. But *what if* you see stress as a friend whose goal is to *help you get ready* for difficult situations, to *protect you from threats and dangers,* and to *challenge you to reach higher?* Perhaps it's not all that bad, right?

It's all about getting to know your stress, when and why it occurs, and ultimately becoming friends with it. Stress's mission is not to destroy you, but to help you out. Studies have found that those who work with stress and embrace it actually live happier lives and aren't any more prone to disease than those who experience minimal stress in life. So, you see...it's better to befriend your stress than to make it an enemy.

DIRECTIONS

It's time to make amends and become friends with your stress. Stop fighting it. For this activity get two different colored pens or pencils. Use one color for "Foe" and the other for "Friend." In the "Foe" space below write all of the negative things that stress does to you. Be sure to include the negative messages it tells you. This should be easy to do because you have been taught how bad stress is for you.

Foe:

In the "Friend" space below write about some positive things that stress can do for you. For example, if you're stressed about a test, rather than thinking that your stress is going to make you forget everything, what if it is trying to motivate you to study and be prepared? What if you're stressed about going out with a group of friends? Are you going to make up an excuse and miss out on the fun? Maybe the stress is just trying to get you the confidence you need to urge you to overcome your fear and have a go and have a good time. Have you ever thought of it that way? Perhaps your stress hasn't been the enemy at all; maybe it's been trying to motivate you to do something even though you thought it was trying to block you.

Friend:

EXPAND ON IT

For the next week, try to shift how you think about your stress; rather than seeing it as an enemy, become friends with it. Each time you feel stress coming on work through the following questions:

What is my stress trying to:

- help me get ready for?

- protect me from?

- help me overcome?

Activity 5.8

OUTSIDE LOOKING IN

INTRODUCTION

If you had a crystal ball and could look into your future, what would you see? How would your life be different from how it is now? Would you be on the honor roll, have a college degree, own a house, or have your dream job? What do you want your future to look like and how is anxiety stopping you from achieving your goals?

In life there are things that you have control over and things you don't. For example, you have no control over your parents' divorce, your father's drinking, your boyfriend's home problems, etc. The reason you lack control is that these things happen because of other people's behaviors and decisions, not yours. You are responsible for your choices and behaviors. Keep your eyes on what you do have the power to change rather than getting stuck on things you can't change. Focus your energy on making positive strides in your life, ones that will lead you towards your vision.

DIRECTIONS

Having a picture of what you want to get out of your life will put you on the right path to living a life that is not controlled by anxiety. When you feel as if you are moving in the right direction you will find that you become more focused on achieving your life goals.

Look at the crystal balls on the next page; one is your life "Now" and the other one is what you want in your "Future," your dreams, aspirations, and goals. In the "Now" crystal ball write what your life currently looks like. In the "Future" ball write down your vision of what you want your life to look like. Cross through the things that you don't have control over in both crystal balls. Put your time and energy into the items that you've circled, because those are the only things that you have the power to change.

170

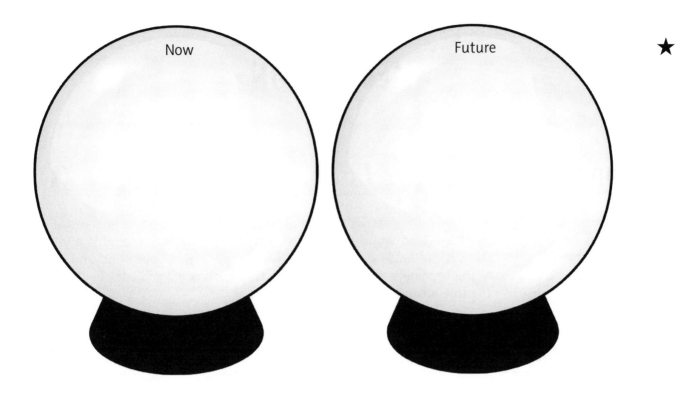

★

EXPAND ON IT

Nothing brings a sense of gratification like a sense of accomplishment. Moving in the right direction increases self-confidence and fulfillment. Look at your crystal balls and answer the questions below:

1. Does your "Now" chart look like your "Future" one? What differences do you notice? Explain.

2. List the behaviors and actions that are keeping your "Now" and "Future" from matching.

3. Describe how changing your behaviors and actions can help you reach your dreams.

MEDITATION

INTRODUCTION

Meditation is a simple way to calm your racing mind, relax your tense body, and find peace in the midst of day-to-day chaos. Meditation cleansing is a way to purify your thoughts and let go of the negativity that you are holding onto. It is a way of detoxifying your mind and soul. Begin meditating today and becoming aware of the things that are holding you back in life. Free yourself and discover the true meaning of peace.

DIRECTIONS

What you'll need:

- strips of paper
- washable markers
- a bowl of water.

On the strips of paper jot down all of the anxious and worrisome thoughts, feelings, and behaviors that play over and over again in your head.

How to meditate:

1. Get a cushion and sit on it.
2. Place the strips of paper and bowl of water in front of you.
3. Cross both legs in the sitting position, with alternate feet resting on top of the thighs.
4. Pull your right foot over your left thigh so it rests on the bend of your knee.
5. The bottom of your foot should face upwards.
6. Place your hands on your knees, palms open and facing upwards.
7. Straighten your spine. Imagine a thread stretching from the top of your head, pulling your back and head straight toward the ceiling in a straight line.
8. Relax your muscles. Focus on relaxing each muscle in your body. Start with the toes and work your way up to the face.
9. Breathe deeply from your abdomen. Take deep breaths from the abdomen and slowly exhale.
10. Listen for silence. Sit, relax, breathe, and be still.

After you have totally relaxed and calmed your mind, take a slip of paper with a worrisome behavior, thought, or feeling on it.

Read the word out loud. Say, "*I will not let (name of behavior/thought/feeling) control me.*"

Drop the slip of paper in the water and watch the words fade. Imagine cleansing yourself of this troublesome issue. Repeat until each troublesome thought is in the water and fading from your life.

End the activity by closing your eyes and letting go of your troubles. Imagine that you are freeing yourself from these issues.

EXPAND ON IT

You can repeat this meditational cleansing exercise any time you feel overwhelmed or burdened by a thought, feeling, or behavior. The more you practice the greater the benefits. Meditation is an excellent way to reduce anxiety and cleanse yourself of stress.

Chapter Six

COPING WITH ANXIETY

Life will throw many obstacles at us. Along life's journey we will stumble and fall. Some of the obstacles we will encounter include setbacks, relapses, and failure. Learn how to turn life's stumbling blocks into stepping stones.

Chapter Contents

Activity 6.1 Thoughts, Emotions, and Actions (TEA)

Activity 6.2 Constructive and Destructive Coping

Activity 6.3 The Weakest Link

Activity 6.4 Worst-Case Scenario

Activity 6.5 Control Issues

Activity 6.6 Life's Roles

Activity 6.7 Masterpiece of Confidence

Activity 6.8 This Too Shall Pass

Chapter objectives

From this chapter you will:

- learn to deal with anxiety, stress, and worry

- explore how your thoughts, feelings, and actions all work together

- learn to let go of the need for control

- explore healthy and unhealthy coping styles

- learn ways to increase your self-confidence

- learn to let the past go and focus on the future.

Pre-/post-scaling questions

Pre-question

In this chapter you will learn to cope with your anxiety. On a scale of 0 to 10, with zero being "none at all" and 10 being "a lot," rate your current ability to cope with anxiety. Plot the score on the grid below.

Post-question

At the beginning of this chapter you rated yourself at a _____ (let them know the pre-score rating). Using the same scale of 0 to 10, with zero being "none at all" and 10 being "a lot," rate where you are currently in your ability to cope with your anxiety. Plot the post-score on the grid below.

Here are some sample follow-up questions that can assist you in comparing and constrasting your client's scores.

- "I noticed that you moved from a '2' to a '7' on the scale. What are some things that contributed to you moving up?"

- "Are there any things that you feel you'd like to work on more in this chapter that would help you move up on the scale?"

- "I noticed that you didn't move up. Was there anything in particular that you wanted to explore in this section that we didn't cover?"

- "What are some things that can help you move up on the scale?"

- "What has helped you cope in the past?"

- "What has not worked in the past?"

- "What was the most helpful thing that you learned from this chapter?"

- "What did you find to be least useful in this chapter?"

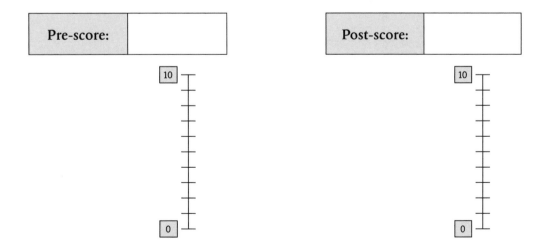

THOUGHTS, EMOTIONS, AND ACTIONS (TEA)

INTRODUCTION

Did you know that your thoughts influence how you feel, which in turn affects how you react in a situation? Understanding your thoughts (T), emotions (E), and actions (A) will help you feel more in control and less anxious.

> Julia was lying in bed playing the day's events over and over in her mind. She was regretting something that she said to a friend. In her mind she played the scenario over and over again. The part that really stood out was her friend angrily staring her in the face and saying "I'll never speak to you again!" Since the incident, Julia has tortured herself for what she has done wrong. It was all her fault that she lost her best friend.

Julia is engaging in a very self-defeating and negative thinking pattern. She has a couple of options: A, continue to berate herself with her thoughts and emotions and avoid situations; B, try something different. Below is an example of her choices for evaluating TEA:

Thoughts	Emotions	Actions
Option A: Failure, idiot, screw-up	Humiliation, shame, anxiety	Avoid school, no sleep
Option B: Made a mistake. I'm not perfect, it'll be okay, I'll fix it tomorrow	Regret, hope, calmness	Go to school and talk to the friend and hope it will work out

Notice how option A is depressing and stressful, but changing a few things and speaking to yourself differently is more uplifting and hopeful.

DIRECTIONS

Look at the following situations. Like Julia's example, work through the situation using the TEA model. Offer two options: A (unhelpful ways to handle) and B (helpful ways to handle).

Kayla really liked a guy and he told her he'd call, but it's been two days and he hasn't.

Thoughts	Emotions	Actions
Option A:		
Option B:		

Joel was getting ready to audition for a large part in the school play. He knew his lines and had practiced for weeks, but now was getting cold feet and feeling extremely anxious.

Thoughts	Emotions	Actions
Option A:		
Option B:		

EXPAND ON IT

For the next week pay attention to how closely related your thoughts, feelings, and actions are. Each time you are faced with a situation that causes anxiety, fear, or stress, record it on the TEA model table and write out options A and B on your table, then record the option you went with. Noticing your TEA patterns will help you change defeating thoughts, emotions, and actions into more positive ones which in turn will affect the outcome of the situation. So you can start working on turning option A into option B!

★

Situation	Thoughts	Emotions	Actions	Option A	Option B	Option chosen

Activity 6.2

CONSTRUCTIVE AND DESTRUCTIVE COPING

★

INTRODUCTION

Coping skills are ways that people deal with life stressors. There are two categories of coping skills: constructive and destructive.

Destructive skills are harmful and can actually make you feel worse. Self-destructive behaviors include things such as cutting, picking at your skin, driving carelessly on purpose, taking drugs or drinking alcohol, and engaging in unprotected sexual activities. While destructive ways of coping may provide temporary relief, they can lead to big problems with major consequences. For example, drinking or taking drugs can become habitual and can lead to an addiction.

Alternatively, constructive or healthy skills are great ways to reduce and alleviate anxiety. They include cooking, playing an instrument, and exercising. It's great to preoccupy yourself with something that you enjoy when you're stressed because it can actually give your mind a break. For example, reading can take a person to a different place and different life for a short time. Video gaming can be helpful if not done in excess. If you play video games for hours and hours to escape reality then that's not a healthy coping skill; but if you play for short periods of time to give your mind a break, then that can be beneficial.

DIRECTIONS

How do you cope with anxiety? Take the quiz to see. Circle all the coping skills that you have used to work through stress and anxiety. Use the blank space at the end to add any others that you have used.

1. Go to sleep.

2. Read a book.

3. Have sex.

4. Listen to music.

5. Cut self.

6. Work out.

7. Eat too much.

8. Play an instrument.

9. Eat too little.

10. Go for long walks.

11. Dwell on dark thoughts.

12. Draw a picture.

13. Pull into isolation and avoid people.

14. Paint a scene or picture.

15. Pick at skin.

16. Talk to someone about the problem.

17. Play video games.

18. Write down thoughts and feelings.

19. Punch something.

20. Cook a meal or dessert.

21. Yell and shout at anyone in the way.

22. Clean.

23. Smoke cigarettes.

24. Watch a movie.

25. Drink a lot of caffeinated beverages.

26. Focus on meditation.

27. Bite nails.

28. Get organized and try to get back in control.

29. Self-medicate with pills, illegal drugs, or alcohol.

30. Go shopping.

31. _____

32. _____

33. _____

34. _____

35. _____

Understanding your responses:

Look at numbers 1–30. How many odd number coping skills did you circle?

How many even number coping skills did you circle?

The odd number skills are unhealthy and destructive ones. The positive number skills are healthy and constructive ones. If you added your own, how many were constructive? How many were destructive?

EXPAND ON IT

Did you circle any unhealthy coping skills? If so, then work through the questions below:

1. Describe how the unhelpful coping skills that you identified are helpful when you're experiencing anxiety.

2. Write the negative consequences that using destructive coping skills can have on you.

3. Of all of the unhealthy coping skills, which is the one you use most often?

Substituting the constructive for the destructive:

List some constructive skills that you can commit to using in place of the destructive ones.
   For the next week when you feel the urge to use a destructive coping skill, come back to this activity and substitute it for a more constructive one.

Activity 6.3

THE WEAKEST LINK

★

INTRODUCTION

'A chain is only as strong as its weakest link'

Thomas Reid

Are you guilty of holding onto thoughts, fears, or emotional baggage? Do these things hold your mind a prisoner to anxiety? Do you feel trapped? If so, don't fret, there is good news...you can break the chains that bind you. Whether it be fear of what people think or losing friends, or fear of failure, these insecurities are deeply rooted. It's important to take a look at where they came from and the purpose they serve; then you can unlock the power they have on your life.

Jared was a 16-year-old who struggled with his anxiety. He had a hard time talking to others about his problems. It's difficult to talk about things you have a hard time understanding yourself. So, needless to say, Jared chose to tuck away his problems and keep them to himself. When they felt too much he'd zone out by playing video games for hours upon hours. Though this strategy didn't make his problems go away, it did take his mind temporarily off them. Jared was becoming a hermit, locking himself away for days on end. His only interaction was with avatars in his games.

One day something happened to his gaming system. He felt as if it was the end of his world, until he remembered that there were some games he could access via the internet. When he turned on his computer his home page was a news media outlet. One of the headlines caught his eye..."Scientists Offer New Insight into Understanding Anxiety." Jared clicked the link to read the article. The article described what anxiety was, the signs and symptoms, and ways to counteract it. After reading the article, Jared felt relieved because he finally knew what he was struggling with.

He started searching for more information about anxiety. He read that sometimes you have to confront your fears to overcome them. So, he decided to identify what was keeping him from interacting with others. Jared followed a strategy from one of the sites he had visited and listed his fears. He had things such as making a fool out of himself, fear of not being liked, fear of being made fun of, and so on. Next, the site explored facing your fears by taking baby steps. So, Jared thought that he could see if his cousin wanted to go shopping. Jared needed a new pair of trainers, but he had been avoiding the shopping center because it was so busy and crowded.

Jared completed his shopping mission and felt great! He conquered his fear, one step at a time. First, he identified his fears, next he made a plan to tackle them, and then he executed his plan. What a breakthrough! The next weekend Jared's cousin called him to see if he wanted to go shopping. Jared reminded himself that he had done it before and could do it again. Although he still was nervous about going out, he knew from the previous experience that he would have a great time.

DIRECTIONS

What you'll need:

- construction paper
- scissors
- markers
- glue.

Cut the construction paper into strips half an inch wide. Cut these strips into five-inch lengths. You'll need a strip of paper for each troublesome thing that you are experiencing. Next on each strip of paper write down what is worrying you. Then for each link paste both ends of a strip together, making a circle. Choose another worry strip through this circle and paste the ends of the second one together, and so on, until you have a link for each worry in your life.

Answer the questions that follow:

List any observations, thoughts and feelings about your chain.

For each worrisome thing list a helpful way that you can overcome it; for example, call friends and go out, or meet at a restaurant for dinner.

Look at your chain. Describe how seeing all of your troubles tied together feels.

Now, tear your chain apart. Imagine tearing yourself away from each troublesome thing. You don't have to let your anxiety hold you prisoner any longer. Chains are meant to be broken and you can find freedom from anxiety. Did you notice how when the chain isn't whole it doesn't seem as big and it appears more manageable?

Look at the pieces of your chain. Describe how it feels to break the chain that binds you.

EXPAND ON IT

In Thomas Reid's *Essays on the Intellectual Powers of Man* (1786) he included this phrase:

> In every chain of reasoning, the evidence of the last conclusion can be no greater than that of the weakest link of the chain, whatever may be the strength of the rest.

Look at the phrase and write down how this phrase applies to you and your anxiety.

You can conquer your anxiety one step at a time. You hold the key, so go ahead and unlock it because your chain is only as strong as the weakest link.

WORST-CASE SCENARIO

INTRODUCTION

Zoe had a job interview at a retail store and was highly anxious. She really needed the job, but her anxiety was getting the best of her. "What if I...stutter, can't talk, freeze up, or my zipper is undone?" These thoughts and many more invaded her every waking minute. "What if I screw up so badly that I blow the chance to get the job?" Zoe really wanted the job. "Maybe if I call and cancel the interview I won't have to worry about 'what ifs' and I won't be a failure either." But she knew that she really needed the extra spending money. No matter how hard Zoe tried she couldn't get her anxious thoughts to stop.

Notice that all Zoe's thoughts were about what could go wrong. Not once did she explore things that may go right, such as how she might:

- ace the interview
- speak articulately
- look impeccable
- get the job on the spot
- start at a higher wage than advertised.

Sometimes anxiety can put the spotlight on the worst possible outcome, which overshadows the good things that may happen. Sure, bad things are going to happen in life, there's no way around that, but guess what? Good things are going to happen too! You have a choice to make; you can go around seeking the glass as half empty or half full. It's guaranteed, if you look for bad things you will find them.

The next time your thoughts tell you that bad things are going to happen, stop and think through these questions. You may just find that a little positive thinking can turn the worst-case scenario around.

1. What's the worst thing that could happen?

2. What's the best thing that could happen?

3. What do I have to lose?

4. What do I have to gain?

5. How can I cope if the worst thing happens?

DIRECTIONS

Look at the scenario below and answer the questions that follow.

Scenario: Can you help me?

Hi, I am Dylan, and I am sitting in a meeting for a scholarship. It's a group interview and we all have to take turns answering the questions in front of a panel of judges. As I listen to the other people talk, they really have it together. They are so smart, so well spoken; there is no way that I can compare. I am really getting anxious because my turn is coming up. I can make it to the door in ten long strides and it's looking inviting. My stomach is turning sommersaults and I feel as if my heart is going to bounce right out of my chest. I have prepared for my part for a long time now, so I know I'm ready. I did make it this far and now it's down to the final candidates, but what if I screw this up? What if my accent comes through, what if people think I'm stupid and unworthy of this money? Can you help me?

Help Dylan work through this situation...

1. What's the worst thing that could happen?

2. What's the best thing that could happen?

3. What does Dylan have to lose?

4. What does Dylan have to gain?

5. How can he cope if the worst thing happens?

Your turn! In the space below write a situation in which you're currently struggling with. Then answer the questions that follow.

Personal scenario

1. What's the worst thing that could happen?

2. What's the best thing that could happen?

3. What do I have to lose?

4. What do I have to gain?

5. How can I cope if the worst thing happens?

EXPAND ON IT

Okay, bad things are going to happen in your life and there's no way around it. Some call it Murphy's Law, but if a worst-case scenario does happen, what can you do? Create a Worst Day Ever (WDE) emergency kit, of course. When you just can't spin a negative to a positive, indulge in a WDE kit and enjoy it. But remember this will pass; it is but a moment in time. So give yourself no more than an hour to wallow in misery and then close up your kit and put it back in safe keeping for the next time you have a WDE.

To create your WDE emergency kit you'll need a box (a shoebox works well). Decorate it and fill it with things that are comforting to you. Next, when you're not in the troughs of a WDE, compose an uplifting letter to yourself, saying that you know that this will soon pass and in the near future it won't feel like the big deal it does now. Put a small notebook in your WDE kit to write the date you visited the kit, the reason why, and once you get through the WDE open the kit back up and write down how everything turned out. This will help to remind you the next time you pull your kit off the shelf that everything will work out okay. Plus, when you go back to your kit for a follow-up post, be sure to restock it if you took something out at the last WDE visit.

Here are some other ideas for things that you can place in your WDE kit:

*   a picture of someone special

*   a chocolate bar

*   a letter of encouragement

*   a favorite poem

*   tissues

*   a book of jokes.

CONTROL ISSUES

★

INTRODUCTION

Some people like to feel in control of what's happening in life. Unfortunately, life doesn't work that way. In reality, there are few things that you have control over. You cannot control everything that happens to you. Actually, the majority of things that happen are entirely out of your control. For example, you have no control over what others say or do, you have no control over what life throws at you, and you have no control over the past. You do, however, have control over how to respond and behave in situations. Letting go of your ability to have control will help you feel free and less anxious.

Lacey was a 16-year-old high school student who had been diagnosed with OCD about a year earlier. She had a problem with things being unclean and out of order. Lacey would spend a lot of time keeping her room impeccable. At home, she felt in control and calm because everything was tidy. However, if she went to someone else's home, she'd often freak out. She could never enjoy her visit because she would feel the need to clean their untidy house for them! Unfortunately, rather than being grateful they often became offended by her cleaning their house. Lacey realized that her need for cleanliness was excessive. Her need for control was becoming too much! Lacey saw a therapist regularly about her OCD and she was helping her recognize things that were in and out of her control. Fortunately, it was beginning to help.

One day her therapist challenged her by asking, "Have you ever thought that the people you're visiting may enjoy the way they live and your need to fix them could be causing them anxiety? The next time you feel compelled to clean up behind someone, try to switch shoes with them. Think about how this would make you feel if the shoe was on the other foot."

Well, the "switch the shoe on the other foot" trick worked. When she saw things from the others' perspective she really began to understand how they may be feeling. Lacey thought, "I would never want someone to experience what I do." With the help of the therapist Lacey started to work on her control issues. Releasing control was not easy, but she was tired of fighting the impossible. Lacey wanted to be able to go somewhere and have fun without feeling the need to fix everything the way that she wanted it.

DIRECTIONS

Look at the following statements and put a tick next to all that you have control over.

- ❑ Washing your laundry.
- ❑ Stopping someone from laughing at you.
- ❑ Cleaning your room.
- ❑ Having a flat tire.
- ❑ Having a picture of you uploaded by someone else online.
- ❑ Doing your homework.
- ❑ Having a dead phone battery.
- ❑ Someone talking about you.
- ❑ Healthy eating.
- ❑ Receiving a text from a friend.
- ❑ Going for a jog.
- ❑ Taking care of your body.
- ❑ Taking prescription medications.
- ❑ Talking back to your parents.
- ❑ Getting good grades.
- ❑ Your dentist being late to your appointment.
- ❑ Being on time.
- ❑ Posting something on your social networking site.
- ❑ Passing a test.
- ❑ Laying your clothes out for school the next day.
- ❑ Your parents fighting.
- ❑ Whether it rains or shines.
- ❑ Your friend standing you up.
- ❑ Your phone not getting service.
- ❑ Having fun when you're out with your friends.

Some of these were easy and some may have been difficult. Many times the line between control and no control can get blurry. The main thing to remember is that if it's within your circle of actions and behaviors, then you control it.

EXPAND ON IT

In the square on the right record things or people that you would like to control in your life, but have no control over.

In the square on the left record some of the things that you do have control over.

Control issues	Self-control

If you put all your time and energy in the "Control issues" square you're setting yourself up for a big disappointment; rather, focus on the area in which you have control. Letting go of control isn't easy. You may find yourself getting anxious about things that you have no control over. When in this situation, ask yourself, "Does this belong in the control issue box or the self-control one?" Focus on what you do have control over in life.

Activity 6.6

LIFE'S ROLES

INTRODUCTION

We are all individuals who carry multiple roles in life, whether it be son or daughter, student, worker, community member, friend, boyfriend/girlfriend, granddaughter, athlete, musician, artist, etc. Each one of these roles is very important. Throughout life, roles change. For example, a student may be a professional in the future. People who have children pick up the role of parent and then their parent takes on the role of grandparent.

The key to having a meaningful and fulfilling life is to find balance and harmony within your roles. To help illustrate this point, look at Terrance's example below.

Terrance's mother was constantly on his case about something. He played what he would like to say to his mother over and over again in his head. "Do this, do that, doesn't she realize that I have other responsibilities. If I don't make time to study I'll never get into a decent school. No wonder I go to school all jittery. She's constantly nagging me about everything that I do wrong and never looks at what I do right." Terrance remembered working with a teacher about trying to resolve conflict between roles. His teacher told him that just as when two people have a conflict, our separate roles can also get into a conflict. One may want to do something another doesn't want to do. A perfect example is the role of friend and student. Many times the friend in us wants to go and have fun, but the student tells us "no" because we have too much to do. This role conflict can cause trouble if you don't mediate and come up with a resolution. Terrance thought this different way of looking at things made a lot of sense. So, he tried to do mediation with what he was currently struggling with. On a piece of paper he worked through his dilemma and then took action.

Role	Responsibilities	Strengths	Weakness	Conflicting role	Level of anxiety
Son	Clean house	Hard worker	Fight with parents	Student	10
Student	Get good grades, take challenging classes	Good student	Don't have time to prepare	Son	7

As you can see from Terrance's example the roles of student (wanting to work on homework) and son (needing to do chores) are in conflict, which contributes to his level of anxiety. Do you have roles that conflict in your life? Do some of your roles produce more anxiety than others? By exploring each of your roles in detail, you can figure out which ones create stress and anxiety and then do some conflict resolution between your roles.

DIRECTIONS

★ On the table below list the following pieces of information.

1. List all the roles that you currently have.

2. List some of the responsibilities of each role.

3. List your strengths in each role.

4. List your weaknesses in each role.

5. Does each role conflict with any other role?

6. On a scale of 1–10, one being "none at all" and 10 being "major anxiety", rate the level of anxiety each role brings to you.

7. What are some strategies that you can do to decrease your anxiety in this role?

Role	Responsibili-ties	Strengths	Weakness	Conflicting role	Level of anxiety

EXPAND ON IT

Answer the questions that follow:

1. Describe the major role conflicts that you observed from your table.

2. List any patterns that you noticed.

3. List any anxiety roles that you can decrease or eliminate. If you do not have any, describe some things you can do to decrease your level of anxiety in the roles.

MASTERPIECE OF CONFIDENCE

INTRODUCTION

Life is like a piece of mosaic art. Each small part creates a beautiful, unique pattern. When you look at each small piece you realize the importance it plays in making up the artwork, but if you look at the pieces individually the art looks fragmented, like a piece of glass. If you think about it, life is a lot like mosaic art; each piece of our life forms part of a beautiful masterpiece. Each one of us carries wonderful strengths and characteristics that make us the individual that we are. No two pieces will ever be the same. No two artists will ever be the same because there's only one artist of this masterpiece...you!

DIRECTIONS

To begin this activity circle all the characteristics that describe you.

Caring	Charismatic	Compassionate	Coordinated
Dependable	Determined	Energetic	Funny
Giving	Honest	Innovative	Smart
Spunky	Strong	Talented	_____
_____	_____	_____	_____

Write as many more as you can think of:

Now you're going to need some art supplies:

- construction paper
- scissors
- marker pens
- glue.

For this activity you get to be creative and have fun. Cut the paper into unique shapes; you will be gluing this onto your mosaic page. On the colorful papers write down all of the wonderful characteristics that you wrote down or circled about yourself. Take your characteristics and glue them in any pattern or design onto a blank piece of paper. Become a Masterpiece of Confidence and remind yourself that you are the artist and you can overcome anything, including anxiety.

EXPAND ON IT

It's important to feel good about yourself. You can do this by celebrating your strengths and you can find your strength in your confidence. Display your artwork in a place that is readily accessible. The next time you find yourself feeling really down, look at your Masterpiece of Confidence and believe in yourself!

THIS TOO SHALL PASS

INTRODUCTION

Change is inevitable in life and what you're feeling now may not even be remembered in the future.

Mackenzie was a 17-year-old girl who had struggled with anxiety since middle school. Many people had tried to help her along the way, but one person really stood out in her memory: her volleyball coach. She once shared something with Mackenzie that would remain with her forever. She said, "When I feel anxious about performing, playing, or anything else in life I tell myself that 'This too shall pass'...and remember Mackenzie, you can do anything for 15 minutes. So in the future if you have to recite a speech, play in a game, or anything else, you can do it."

One day Mackenzie had to do something that she was equally excited and yet nervous about. She was afraid that her anxiety would hold her back and keep her from doing it, but she was determined not to let her anxiety hold her back this time. So, she went for it. Each time Mackenzie felt anxiety creeping into her mind she told herself, "This too shall pass. You can do anything for 15 minutes, or half an hour, or even an hour, for that matter. Because that's just a brief moment in time and it too shall pass." She did it and it worked. Just like Mackenzie, you too can do anything you set your mind to for a brief moment in time!

DIRECTIONS

Life is ever-changing. It is ebbing and flowing with joy and sorrow, fear and courage, and anger and peace; nothing is constant, but it is ever-changing. Try this...find a comfortable place and reflect on the things that are going on in your life at this moment in time. Be careful not to put more emphasis on the bad. So if you find yourself gravitating toward the bad things first, think of some good ones as well. Write them down. If there is a time constraint on an item you have listed, put this beside your entry. For example, if this event will be off your list in a week, then write one week beside it. After each event write the following words: "This too shall pass... I can do anything or overcome anything for this moment in time."

EXPAND ON IT

Spend some time meditating on each of the items you wrote down. Take deep abdominal breaths as you reflect on each entry. Try not to let your mind get ahead of you and start thinking in the future; stay right here in the present.

After focusing on each event repeat aloud to yourself: "This too shall pass... I can do anything or overcome anything for this moment of time."

The key to making this exercise work is your belief that this moment in time shall pass. Moments are not eternity; they are only small snapshots of what's happening in life right here and right now.

Chapter Seven

ALLEVIATING ANXIETY

Change is a choice. As the saying goes, "You are not what you think you are but what you think, you are" (Norman Vincent Peale). So to change old patterns you must change how you think, which in turn changes how you act.

Chapter contents

Chapter objectives

From this chapter you will:

- learn to take some time out of your day to appreciate your life

- learn to take a compliment and give yourself a pat on the back

- explore how to give your racing mind a break, or better yet a vacation

- learn how to relax

- explore where peace is found

- find relaxation through music

- learn to live a rich, fulfilling, and meaningful life that is not anxiety driven.

Pre-/post-scaling questions

Pre-question

As everything comes to a close, you will tie all the pieces of what you have learned together. This chapter explores ways to find peace in your life amid anxiety. On a scale of 0 to 10 with zero being "none at all" and 10 being "a lot," rate how much peace you feel in your life right now. Plot the score on the grid below.

Post-question

At the beginning of this chapter you rated yourself at a _____ (let them know the pre-score rating). Using the same scale of 0 to 10, with zero being "none at all" and 10 being "a lot," rate where you are currently in how much peace you feel in your life. Plot the post-score on the grid below.

Here are some sample follow-up questions that can assist you in comparing and contrasting your client's scores.

- "I noticed that you moved from a '2' to an '8' on the scale. What are some things that contributed to you moving up?"

- "Are there any things that you feel you'd like to work on more in this chapter that would help you move up on the scale?"

- "I noticed that you didn't move up. Was there anything in particular that you wanted to explore in this section that we didn't cover?"

- "What are some things that can help you move up on the scale?"

- "Where do you find peace?"

- "What was the most helpful thing that you learned from this process?"

- "In comparison to when you started, how far do you think you have come in your ability to cope with anxiety?"

- "What tools will you take with you as you leave therapy?"

- "Where would you like to go from here?"

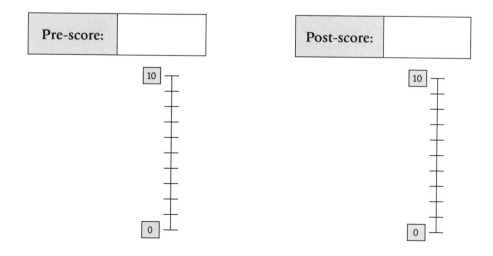

DO SOMETHING DIFFERENT TODAY

INTRODUCTION

Have you ever been stuck doing the same thing over and over again? Anxiety is notoriously popular for keeping you stuck in uncomfortable situations. A terrific way to break free is to "do something different" and do something new and exciting.

Derek shared a couple of his journal entries to show how he broke free of the monotony of social anxiety.

Saturday at 10am

I am so bored. This social anxiety disorder is kicking my butt. I am sick and tired of locking myself up in my house because I'm afraid that I will be judged by others. My parents tried to get me to go with my sister and her friends to the movies last night, but I just couldn't make myself do it. I really wanted to see the movie too! I feel like a complete failure. How do I break this cycle and actually do what I want to? I am so sick of letting my anxiety control me!

Saturday at 1:00pm

Just read a cool article called "Take the Challenge: Do Something Different." It was about changing your normal routine and adding some spice to your life. So, why not give it a try? The first thing I have to do is identify something that I really want to do... Easy, try my new board out at the new skate park. I've been dying to give it a try, but my fear of making a fool out of myself, and everyone seeing it, kept me from doing it. But that's going to change. I asked my sister to give me a lift to the park and I am leaving in a few minutes. I am so nervous, but I am not turning back—game on.

Saturday at 4pm

I did it! Just got back from the park and it was awesome! Even though I sat on a bench with my sister for half an hour before making myself do it, once I got on the ramp I felt free. I even had a cool group of guys stop and watch some of my moves and ask for pointers and tips. I am going to meet up with my new friends at the park next Saturday. I am still nervous, but my sister said she'd go with me. Having her there as a support really helps!

Tomorrow's challenge: learn to play the electric guitar; Mom is really going to love that one!

DIRECTIONS

Take the "Do something different today" challenge. Begin by identifying something that you have always wanted to do, but didn't have the courage or confidence, and go and do it. Be sure to choose an activity that doesn't involve something unsafe. Record your activities on the chart and mark them off when you accomplish the challenge. It's important to challenge yourself and do things that make you feel good. This is especially true if you're working on defeating anxiety.

Day	Activity	Feeling before	Completed	Feeling after
Sunday				
Monday				
Tuesday				
Wednesday				
Thursday				
Friday				
Saturday				

EXPAND ON IT

You can continue to take the challenge every day of your life. The "Do something different today" challenge is a great way to push you out of your comfort zone and do something you wouldn't dare to do otherwise. You have nothing to lose by taking the challenge, but you may have a lot to gain!

COMPLIMENTS

INTRODUCTION

A compliment is a gesture of honor, a sign of respect, admiration, and well wishes. Compliments are given, but how are they received? How well do you receive compliments? Are you more prone to accept something negative than positive? Do you take the compliment and appreciate it, feel good, and offer gratitude back or do you discount the compliment and think you aren't worthy of it?

Anxiety can strip away and discredit good things in life. People with anxiety often discredit compliments and feel awkward when they receive them. They don't feel worthy of the praise and shun it off with a "no problem" or "no big deal," even if they worked really hard for something. They also may feel as if the person giving the compliment is just trying to be nice and polite. That's simply not true—compliments are something to be given and taken.

How do you take a compliment? Follow these quick tips on understanding and accepting a compliment and use them the next time you are offered praise.

Taking a compliment

How to take a compliment

Are you uncomfortable receiving compliments? Do you discount compliments when they are given? By not accepting a compliment the giver may stop giving them to you. There are several ways that people deflect a compliment, for example suggesting that anyone could have done what you did, thinking that the giver wants something from you in return, getting overly awkward and embarrassed, giving a compliment back immediately, or brushing it off as if the giver doesn't mean it. Each of these ways not only puts you down but also your giver. Learn to acknowledge and appreciate the gift of a compliment. Often, just by accepting a compliment you are returning a gift of gratitude to your giver.

Five "Don't" tips when receiving a compliment

- Don't make up excuses as to why you don't deserve the compliment.
- Don't try to over analyze the compliment. Accept the kind words with gratitude and move on.
- Don't tell yourself you are not worthy of the compliment.
- Don't dismiss the compliment. If they took time to say it, it meant something to them.
- Don't discredit the compliment by telling yourself you aren't special or anyone could have done what you did.

How to accept a compliment

There are many ways that you can accept a compliment. Here are the three basic "S"s of accepting a compliment: *smile* and keep your reply *short* and *simple*. Here are some tips to accepting it in a positive way:

- First things first, say "Thank you."

- For example: "Thanks, I appreciate that" or "Thanks, that really means a lot to me."

- For a more in depth thank you, try something like this: "Thank you. I'm glad you noticed that I've worked really hard on it" or "Thanks. I tried really hard."

- Think about the compliment and what you did really well to receive it.

- Store the compliment in your mind, write it down, or text it to yourself as a reminder of the positive things people notice about you.

How to return a compliment

It's nice to pay compliments back, but don't feel as if you have to do it on the heels of their compliment or it may not appear sincere. When you give a compliment you want it to be genuine and not as if you have to give one just because you received one. However, if you do have a genuine respect to pay then do so. Whether you are acknowledging how nice they are or how good their compliment made you feel, be friendly and genuine and the rest will come naturally.

DIRECTIONS

Practice genuinely accepting the compliments below and write your response to the compliment on the line.

- Your presentation was the best in the class.

- You can really draw!

- I love your outfit!

- I wish that I had hair like yours.

- You made these? They are awesome!

- You are so nice. I wish I was as kind as you.

- How do you keep so organized? I am so jealous.

- You are super talented.

- You are a natural born leader. It's awesome how everyone looks up to you.

- I really enjoyed reading your blog. I connected to it.

Add a few compliments that you have received and write a response back using the tips from this activity.

EXPAND ON IT

Answer the questions below:

1. Describe how you feel when you receive a compliment.

2. How do you usually respond to a compliment?

3. Do you give compliments to others?

4. Describe a time when you paid someone a compliment and he/she blew it off. How did you feel?

Practice, practice, practice taking compliments over and over again in a mirror until you feel confident in compliment accepting. Then over the course of the next week, try out accepting and responding to compliments. Remember, you receive compliments when someone admires something you have done. They are not just empty words, but something that the giver wants to share with you, and what an honor that is!

MENTAL VACATION

INTRODUCTION

The human mind is a powerful thing. It is constantly searching for answers, trying to resolve problems, and conjuring up things. Even when you're asleep, it's still busy at work. The mind is a non-resting part of who you are. It stores your personality and it makes you, you. People often take the mind for granted and forget to give it a break. The mind loves to daydream, doodle, and venture off every now and then. When is the last time that you let your mind take a vacation?

Your mind tries to take a vacation each time you rest or meditate. In fact, it finds comfort in those times. Even if you can't physically go on a vacation you can go on a mental one and this type of vacation doesn't take any preparation, planning, or packing.

Read Jada's story below where she goes to find peace. Notice how all her senses are at work while she's there; she isn't missing a single detail, but rather absorbing everything around her.

Jada had a really bad day. She felt very nervous about her driving test tomorrow. "I really need a vacation," she thought. She remembered an activity that she did at summer camp one time called mental vacation. She took out her phone and uploaded some ocean sounds. Then she took a deep breath and sat on the edge of her bed. Jada closed her eyes and let her mind take her to the beach, one of her favorite vacation spots. Soon the cotton sheet on her bed became a crisp white blanket of sand. The plush carpet underneath her feet became the cool ocean water and she imagined sea mist spraying on her face. She envisioned picking up a handful of sand and feeling the small grainy texture slip through the crevices of her fingers. The warm tropical winds blew strands of hair out of her face. The fresh smell of the ocean soothed her soul. Jada could hear the waves sing their sweet song back and forth. As the tide rolled in and the tide rolled out it reminded her of life. She tasted a hint of sea salt as she deeply inhaled the fresh air. Tranquility and peace were consuming her. When Jada opened her eyes, she felt refreshed...like a new person. "Sometimes you just need to get away," she thought.

DIRECTIONS

Where is your mental vacation spot? In the space below create a description of a special place you would like to visit. This place should be a place that is relaxing and calm. It can be a place that you have been to before or one that you'd like to visit. Describe your vacation destination in detail. Be sure to include the five senses (tasting, touching, hearing, seeing, and smelling) in your description, and be as graphic as possible.

Answer the questions below:

1. Describe how you felt before doing this exercise.

2. Describe what you experienced with each of your senses.
    Hearing

    Seeing

    Smelling

    Touching

    Tasting

3. Describe how you felt after completing this exercise.

4. Describe how taking a mental vacation can help you escape an anxious moment.

EXPAND ON IT

Collect mementos, pictures, or souvenirs of places that you like to go or would like to visit. For example, if it's the beach you may chose a seashell or a postcard of the ocean or a souvenir that you bought from one of your vacations at the beach, or you can even draw your memory! Put your item in a place where you will see it often. Use it as a constant reminder to stop and give yourself a break, a mental vacation. Try to do this activity at least once a week.

Activity 7.4

PROGRESSIVE MUSCLE RELAXATION

INTRODUCTION

Studies have shown that teens who meditate experience reduced levels of stress. Mindfulness is acting in the here and now and focusing on emotions, sensations, and feelings that you are currently experiencing. When you go into a mindful zone your body reacts by becoming less tense and your muscles respond by relaxing; your breathing becomes fuller which in turn affects your relaxation level.

There is another technique in mindfulness to help you relax that involves focusing on your muscles and then relaxing them one by one. This technique is known as Progressive Muscle Relaxation or PMR. It's super easy to do and you don't need materials to do it. It's a great way to calm down and reduce anxiety.

DIRECTIONS

Here are the steps to follow to do PMR:

1. Lie on a comfortable surface.

2. Take a couple of deep abdominal breaths.

3. Close your eyes.

4. At your toes begin tensing your body, slowly working up your legs, your abdomen, chest, your shoulders, your arms, neck, and face; clench your jaw, scrunch your eyes and forehead.

5. Once your body is completely tense hold for a few seconds. Feel the tension throughout your body.

6. Then as slowly as you tensed your body, allow the tension to drain out of you. Start with your forehead and your eyes, unclench your jaw, relax your face and neck. Let the tension drain from your shoulders and arms until they become limp; release your chest and abdomen and let it go from your legs all the way to your toes until you feel like a rag doll.

7. Take a couple of deep abdominal breaths.

8. Open your eyes.

You have just completed an exercise in PMR.
   Answer the questions below:

1. Describe how you felt before doing PMR.

2. Describe how you felt during it.

3. Describe how you felt after PMR.

4. Explain how you can use this activity to help you relax.

EXPAND ON IT

Make a meditation schedule for the next week. Write the type of meditation you will do and how long you will do it each time.

Day	Type of meditation	How long?	How you felt	
			Before	After
Sunday				
Monday				
Tuesday				
Wednesday				
Thursday				
Friday				
Saturday				

Through the course of your journey you have learned several relaxation techniques from deep breathing, seated position meditation, visualization, mental vacations, and now PMR. Of the various ways you have learned to meditate, which one is your favorite?

RIGHT HERE AND NOW

INTRODUCTION

With the past, I have nothing to do; nor with the future. I live now.

Ralph Waldo Emerson

Stay in the past, worry about the future, or make a change? It's up to you. Right here, right now...that's all you've got. Today is everything. You've made a commitment to change how you respond to anxiety. Don't let yourself be at the same place next year. If you want to change, it's up to you. Tomorrow isn't a guarantee and all you've got is right here and right now, today.

Go ahead, make future plans, don't worry about yesterday—all that is certain in life is this moment. Don't let it pass you by without acknowledging it. If you want to change, you can turn this thing around. What are you waiting for?

DIRECTIONS

Complete the statements below and answer the questions that follow.

Things that hold me to the past:

Things I worry about in the future:

In your answers for both of the above areas, circle what you have control over. Odds are there are a lot of things that you don't have control over, yet you worry yourself sick about them. Look at the items you circled. Those are the things that are happening right now, things that you can change.

Now, imagine you have one gigantic eraser and you are erasing the areas that you don't have control over completely from your life.

Describe what you would erase first. List how that item is affecting your life and how you would feel if it were completely gone.

Letting these things go is entirely up to you. One way to let something go visually is to get a balloon and have a moment of release. Read aloud "I am freeing myself from...(name each item you are holding onto) then let the balloon go. Let the past things go with it. It's time to live right here and right now.

EXPAND ON IT

List the things that you have to do today.

Things that I have to face today:

This is all that you have to focus on right now. You may be thinking, "I have a project due on Friday." Okay, then plan to do a little of it today, but assuming all of the stress for a project due in a few days today is just going to stress you out. Do some of it today, then repeat this exercise tomorrow and do a little more tomorrow. By Friday, your project will be done. You don't have to tackle everything at once. That will just get you all stressed out; you can take small steps and the small ones will lead you to the same end result.

If you worry about what might be, and wonder what might have been, you will ignore what is.

Unknown

Activity 7.6

INNER PEACE

INTRODUCTION

Inner peace is something we all strive to have in life, especially those who struggle with anxiety. Inner peace is the serenity, tranquility, and a sense of connectedness when we feel at one with ourselves. It is within all of us if we just open our eyes, heart, and soul to it. It is easier to get caught up in the chaos that life brings, than to be quiet and focus on the positives that surround us. There is a simple child quote that reminds us to "take time to smell the flowers." It goes something like this:

Take some time along the way

To see what's nice about today.

When was the last time you put your mind at ease? When is the last time you stopped to smell the flowers or took some time out of your day to focus on the good things surrounding you? More importantly, when is the last time you felt at peace?

DIRECTIONS

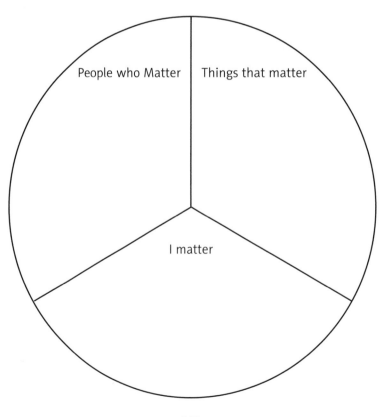

Inside each section of the Peace symbol write the following information:

People who matter: List people who mean a lot to you in life. These can be friends, role models, parents, and/or family members.

Things that matter: List things that you enjoy in life. These can include special things you do to bring your enjoyment, such as tennis, reading, sewing, sketching, writing, etc. These are things that would be missing in your life if you didn't have them, or do them.

"I" matter: List the characteristics that make you who you are. Think of your talents, things that you are good at, and things that set you apart from others. From being witty to being organized, these are the things that make you, you!

People Who Matter

Look at the people you listed on the Peace symbol. On a separate piece of paper for each person write the following information:

- Person's name

- What makes him/her an important part of your life?

- How often do you let him/her know the impact he/she has on your life?

Things that matter

Look at the things you listed on the Peace symbol. Write the following information:

- List the item that means the most to you on your list.

- Describe its importance in your life.

- How often do you do it?

"I" matter

Look at the characteristics you listed on your Peace symbol. Write the following information:

- List the characteristic that you value most about yourself.

- Describe the significance this characteristic has on your life.

- How often do you focus on the positive traits that you have?

EXPAND ON IT

Take a meditational moment to focus deeply on your circle of peace. Each item you listed holds significance for your happiness and success in life. While the search for inner peace is a daily quest, when you find it you will find the true meaning of tranquility and harmony. Inner peace does lie within you. Only you hold the key to unlocking the door to yours. Your peace diagram is a map of what and who you need in your life to reach your own serenity. Good luck on your journey and peace be with you.

LIFE SONG

★

INTRODUCTION

Music is a wonderful therapeutic tool to help you get through difficult times. Music has been shown to stimulate brainwaves (they change to resonate with the beat) which changes mood and even behavioral responses, depending on the type of music you're listening to. For example, music with a fast, upbeat tempo can improve concentration and alertness, while music with a slower tempo produces calmness and a meditative state. Plus, the benefits continue long after the music stops. When your brainwaves shift, other neat things start happening in your body, for example your muscles relax, you become more alert, and your breathing and heart rate alter.

Music is also known to inspire people to work. A gym class is the perfect example of how music is used to motivate and relax. In most classes you'll hear upbeat and fast-tempo music playing during cardio or an aerobic activity because it revs the class up and inspires them to work to the beat. Conversely, at the end of class there is usually a cool-down period where you will hear slow low-tempo music playing. This helps the class relax and get the heart back to a resting rate.

There are a lot of benefits to listening to music. Here are just a few:

- reduces stress

- eases anxiety

- decreases depression

- promotes relaxation

- increases concentration

- boosts the immune system

- decreases blood pressure

- elevates mood

- alleviates pain.

With all of those benefits, crank up the tunes.

DIRECTIONS

 Describe the type of music you listen to.

What is your favorite song?

Describe what makes that song so special to you.

What is another song that you like?

Describe what makes this song special.

Are there any themes in the music that you listen to? If so, describe them.

Find a quiet place free of distractions and listen to a fast, upbeat song that you like. After you listen to it write down how it felt listening to that song.

Next, find a slow-tempo song that you enjoy. After you listen to it write down how it felt listening to that song.

EXPAND ON IT

Imagine that you're a musician—rock, country, alternative, R&B, rap, screamo, it doesn't matter, take your pick. Write the lyrics to your own song.

Title:

Verse 1:

Chorus:

Verse 2:

Chorus:

Verse 3:

Chorus:

You can use music anytime in your life when you're feeling down and when you're feeling great. It doesn't matter because music is always around and it's a great way to get through life's difficulties.

VALUES, GOALS, AND ACTIONS

INTRODUCTION

Are you living a life consistent with your values? Life is too short not to live a life that's not in line with what you believe and value. You may recall the Values Compass you did at the beginning of your journey. Values are what we treasure in life. We all have them and they are different for everyone. They give our lives direction and meaning. Values are not goals. Goals can be achieved but values are the foundation of our goals. Goals are something that you want to shoot for in life. Both are important in finding inner peace and happiness.

There are six steps to setting and achieving a goal.

1. Define your goal.

2. Identify steps to achieve it.

3. Write out the steps in sequence.

4. Make a commitment to each step.

5. Take each step regardless of how you feel. No excuses.

6. Reward yourself every time you conquer a step.

The anxious mind will create roadblocks and barriers to keep you from achieving your goals and living out your values. It will tell you that you're not good enough or smart enough, and that you won't succeed. You don't have to listen to that anxious mind! It's just spinning negativity all around you. You can take those thoughts and spin them in the opposite direction. You can even change them if you wish.

Once you set some goals that are in line with your values and work toward them you'll be amazed at how great you will feel, and when you feel good you accomplish great things!

DIRECTIONS

Record your values below. If your values have not changed you can use the ones you listed on your Values Compass.

Identify three goals that you would like to achieve. Keep your goals realistic. For example, a goal to become a superhero with non-human strength is not a realistic or achievable goal, but taking a speech course to help you overcome speaking in front of people is. Make sure your goal is reachable and realistic. Record the steps you will take to reach your goal. Identify any obstacles or barriers that you'll face in achieving it. Next, think of different strategies that you can use to overcome the obstacle. Don't forget to reward yourself for completing each step. Your reward can be anything from downloading a song that you have been wanting, to going to see a movie. You get to choose the reward. Last but not least, be sure to tick the goal off your list when you've achieved it. An example has been provided.

First goal	Steps	Obstacles	Strategies	Success	Rewards
Spend more time with friends.	1. Make time twice a week for friends. Put birthdays and hangout times on my calendar.	Stress over and fear going out in public.	Use online calendar more to remind me via phone.	X	Get new app for phone.
	2. Return calls and texts from friends.	No time and a bad habit of not talking to anyone.	Make a time each day to return calls and texts.	X	Watch favorite show after I return calls.

Complete the table for each goal.

First goal	Steps	Obstacles	Strategies	Success	Rewards

★

Second goal	Steps	Obstacles	Strategies	Success	Rewards

Third goal	Steps	Obstacles	Strategies	Success	Rewards

You will be setting goals for the rest of your life. You can use this simple chart to help you keep on track each time you set one.

EXPAND ON IT

Look at the list of values and mark the ones that you value not only in yourself, but also in others. Do not put too much thought into it. If the word jumps off the page at you, then mark it.

Acceptance	Diligence	Hope	Relaxation
Accomplishment	Eagerness	Humor	Responsibility
Advancement	Empathy	Hygiene	Security
Agility	Ethics	Independence	Self-control
Approval	Fairness	Individuality	Selflessness
Artistry	Faith	Inspiration	Serenity
Balance	Fame	Integrity	Sexuality
Beauty	Family	Justice	Sincerity
Belonging	Fashion	Knowledge	Skillfulness
Calmness	Fearlessness	Logic	Solitude
Carefulness	Fitness	Maturity	Spirituality
Change	Flexibility	Mellowness	Structure
Commitment	Freedom	Motivation	Teamwork
Compassion	Friendliness	Optimism	Trustworthiness
Competition	Gratitude	Patience	Uniqueness
Courtesy	Happiness	Peace	Virtue
Decisiveness	Health	Perseverance	
Dependability	Holiness	Persistence	
Determination	Honesty	Pride	

Look at the values that you marked; describe any patterns that you observe.

Describe why it is important to live a life in accordance with your values.

POST-THERAPY ANXIETY PROFILE

INTRODUCTION

You began this process by creating an Anxiety Profile in Activity 1.5. Sometimes, we don't give ourselves credit where it is due. Have you stopped to think about where you started your journey and where you are now? Celebrations are important. Take time to take a first-hand look at your journey. While you have come a long way, you still have a long way to go, but at least you have the tools to continue your journey. You may encounter obstacles and setbacks in your journey, but don't let that keep you from moving forward. Rest assured you have everything you need to make it through any obstacle that comes your way.

DIRECTIONS

Read each statement and answer "yes" or "no." Since I have worked through counseling and these activities...

1. I worry less about things.

2. I have slept better using some of the strategies that I have learned.

3. I have noticed a positive change in my eating habits since working on anxiety.

4. I do not panic as often.

5. I am more able to communicate my feelings to others.

6. Others have commented that they have noticed a positive difference in my behavior.

7. I have support systems to help me work through my feelings.

8. I am not as hard on myself as I used to be.

9. I don't worry so much about what others think of me.

10. I am more open to trying things.

11. I don't obsess over things like I once did.

12. I don't let my anxiety stop me from accomplishing things in life.

Circle the number that best describes you.

1. Compared to when I first began therapy, I have noticed an improvement in my ability to control my anxiety.

Please circle only one answer.

1	2	3	4	5
Strongly disagree	Disagree	Neutral	Agree	Strongly agree

2. I will be able to use the techniques and skills from therapy in my everyday life.

Please circle only one answer.

1	2	3	4	5
Strongly disagree	Disagree	Neutral	Agree	Strongly agree

3. I feel more confident in my ability to handle anxiety than when I first started therapy.

Please circle only one answer.

1	2	3	4	5
Strongly disagree	Disagree	Neutral	Agree	Strongly agree

Understanding your profile results

Take a look at your responses. Look how far you've come in your journey compared with when you first began therapy. Go back to Activity 1.5 and compare your answers with those you first gave.

EXPAND ON IT

You have done a wonderful job learning to manage your anxiety. You have climbed a mountain and come a long way. Take time to reflect on your journey and answer the questions below:

1. Looking over your Anxiety Profile in Activity 1.5 and the one you just completed, describe the positive changes that you have undergone.

2. If any, list the negative changes that you have undergone.

3. Describe how you can address the areas that still need work.

4. List something that you wanted to accomplish in therapy but didn't.

5. List the things that you set out to accomplish and did so.

IT'S MY LIFE

INTRODUCTION

Congratulations! You have come to the end of this journey. Though your life journey continues, it is hoped that you have discovered who you are, found strength that you didn't realize you possessed, and have learned to experience peace. Most importantly, you have learned that you hold everything you need within you to conquer anxiety. Take a walk down memory lane to see just how far you have come.

DIRECTIONS

The letter below addresses all of the components you learned in these activities. Step by step you identified sources of your anxiety, challenged self-defeating thoughts, experienced living in the here and now, and explored areas that were not fun about yourself, all while exercising courage and determination each step of the way. Complete the letter by filling in the blanks with your personal takeaways. After you finish the letter, read it aloud, and you may just be surprised at all that you've accomplished. Congratulations!

This is me (your name)

I am a teen who is conquering anxiety. I have struggled with anxiety for (how long). I decided to overcome my anxiety because (list reason). So, I began a journey to conquer it on (start date). I hoped this journey would bring me (enter what you wanted to achieve). Anxiety makes me feel (list the negatives anxiety does to you), but no more. I am taking my life back and here are the things that will help me do it...

This is what I value most in life (list your values)...

These are my goals...

These are the people whom I can lean on when I feel anxious...

★

During this journey I have learned that anxiety affects me in many different ways. Here are some of the ways anxiety affects me and how I take care of myself when I feel I am becoming anxious:

Anxiety affects me:

Body
How I can take care of myself...

Thoughts
How I can take care of myself...

Emotions
How I can take care of myself...

Behaviors
How I can take care of myself...

★

Interpersonally—how I feel about myself
How I can take care of myself...

Here are some of the things that I learned that I will take with me on my anxiety journey...

These are some coping strategies that I can use when I feel anxious...

When I feel anxious it helps to be mindful. Here are some ways that I can practice mindfulness...

One of the favorite things that I learned was...

One of the hardest things I learned to do was...

Here are some things that I still need to work on...

Here is something that I didn't think that I could do, but I did...

One of my biggest accomplishments on this journey was...

★

I am (your name). I am not controlled by anxiety and I will not let it define who I am...

Signature and date

★

This Award is to certify that:

_____
(Name)

Has successfully completed the Anxiety Program.

On: (day, month, day, year) _____ / _____ / _____

Part III

CONCLUSIONS

You have reached the end of this treatment guide and should be nearing the termination of therapy. This is time for a transition that should be characterized by a sense of accomplishment, pride, calmness, and health for the client. A positive termination can be achieved by having open discussions, preferably a few weeks prior to the final session. During this discussion it is important to speak with your client about how far he/she has come in the therapeutic process. As termination can instill anxiety, you will want to make sure that you work your client through the process slowly. Scheduling a follow-up session a few weeks out may help your client feel more comfortable in saying goodbye.

Another way to ensure that your client is moving toward termination is to use the section on charting progress to help him/her gauge the level of readiness. In this final section you can chart your client's progress chapter by chapter and see where and when the most growth occurred. If you plan to use this guide in other sessions or groups, it is recommended to make copies of the "Charting Progress" pages to keep in your client's file. In the "Charting Progress" section there is a sample charting progress graph with an interpretation of results.

There is also the pre- and post-assessment profile that was taken in Chapter 1 and again in Chapter 7. Use this assessment to provide you with information on specific changes that your client has made. Again, you can use these charts and data to share with your client, other approved healthcare providers, and parents. Use these tools to collect information and analyze results. This will help you gain a better understanding of your client's specific needs, allowing you to make appropriate modifications if needed. Both the charting progress graph and the pre- and post-assessment profiles serve as resourceful accountability tools to help you demonstrate your client's progress in therapy.

Following the Charting Progress section are the books and scholarly journal articles used to compile this treatment guide. These resources are provided in the event that you want to expand your knowledge in any of the areas covered in the book. Last, are internet-based resources pertaining to the treatment of anxiety, Cognitive Behavioral Associations and resources and Acceptance Commitment Therapy resources.

It is my sincere hope that you have found *Teen Anxiety* useful and easy to use. I hope that you have observed and experienced the effectiveness in the activities written in this treatment guide. By combining both CBT and ACT, you can feel confident that you have provided your client with the most effective and empirically supported therapeutic approaches in the field.

On a final note, do not underestimate your role. Single handedly, the therapist plays one of the most important roles in therapy. The rapport, trust, and knowledge that you have will be the leading force in helping your client. As stated before, this treatment guide is not a cookbook for anxiety management, but rather a guide to be used at your professional discretion. Thank you for using these activities to assist you in your treatment of teen anxiety.

Charting progress

Use the information from the pre- and post-scaling questions in each chapter and plot it on the chart. The graph will serve as a visual representation of your client's growth through each area addressed in the book. It is hoped that you were able to keep a record of this information as your client progressed throughout therapy. A directory of the chapters is listed below:

- Defining and Understanding Anxiety

- Anxiety and the Body

- Anxiety and Thoughts

- Anxiety and Emotions

- Anxiety and Behavior

- Coping with Anxiety

- Alleviating Anxiety

Sample chart

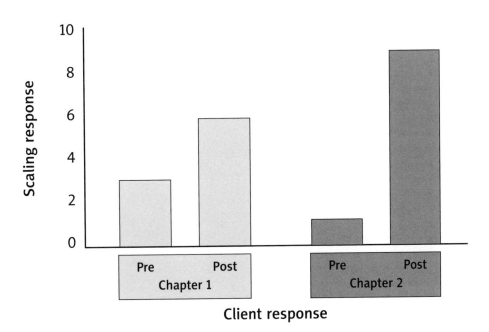

From the chart it is clear that the client experienced the most growth in the chapter relating to anxiety and the body. What caused this amount of growth to occur? How did your client change his/her life based on what he/she learned? Was it how the information was presented or was it the content covered? These are important questions to delve into with your client. Knowing this information can assist you in future sessions. The "Charting Progress" section will help you not only to understand your client but also to see where he/she is gaining the most useful information from therapy. Now, of course, clients will progress, remain stable, or may even go backward during therapy. All stages of therapy deserve further explanation. So use your clinical skills to explore variations of scaling responses.

232

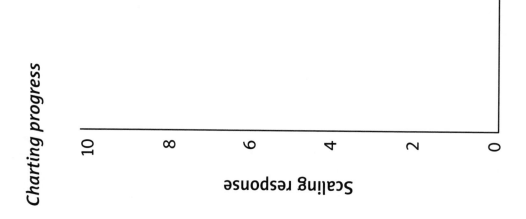

Charting progress

Client response

Pre- and Post-assessments

Review the Anxiety Profile pre- and post-results. The pre-profile results can be found in Activity 1.5. and the post-profile results are in Activity 7.9. It is recommended that copies of both of these assessments be kept for your personal records. Use the self-reported information to measure your client's growth in therapy and any additional strategies that are needed to help your client transition out of therapy.

Compare and contrast

Pre-assessment	Post-assessment

Clinician notes and observations

_____

_____

_____

_____

_____

_____

_____

_____

_____

_____

_____

Homework log

Record your homework for each week on the chart below.

Days of week	Activity	What you thought	How you felt	Impact it made
Sunday				
Monday				
Tuesday				
Wednesday				
Thursday				
Friday				
Saturday				

REFERENCES

Diagnostic and Statistical Manual of Mental Disorders: DSM-IV-TR (2000). Washington, DC: American Psychiatric Association.

Diagnostic and Statistical Manual of Mental Disorders: DSM-5 (2013). Washington, DC: American Psychiatric Association.

Aderka, I., McLean, C., Huppert, J., Davidson, J., and Foa, E. (2013) "Fear, avoidance and physiological symptoms during cognitive-behavioral therapy for social anxiety disorder." *Behaviour Research and Therapy, 51*(7), 352–358.

American Academy of Child and Adolescent's Facts for Families (2008) Available at https://eclkc.ohs.acf. hhs.gov/hslc/tta-system/ehsnrc/docs/_34_Stages_of_adolescence1.pdf, accessed on 12 November 2014.

Arch, J. J. and Craske, M. G. (2008) "Acceptance and commitment therapy and cognitive behavioral therapy for anxiety disorders: Different treatments, similar mechanisms?" *Clinical Psychology: Science & Practice 5*, 263–279.

Arch, J., Eifert, G., Davies, C., Vilardaga, J., Rose, R., and Craske, M. (2012) "Randomized clinical trial of cognitive behavioral therapy (CBT) versus acceptance and commitment therapy (ACT) for mixed anxiety disorders." *Journal of Consulting and Clinical Psychology, 80*(5), 750–765.

Beck, J. S. (2011) *Cognitive Behavior Therapy, Second Edition: Basics and Beyond.* New York, NY: The Guilford Press.

Beck, J. S. (1995) Cognitive Therapy: Basics and beyond. New York: Guilford Press.

Batanova, M. and Loukas, A. (2011) "Social anxiety and aggression in early adolescents: Examining the moderating roles of empathic concern and perspective taking." *Journal of Youth & Adolescence 40*(11), 1534–1543.

Casey, B. J., Ruberry, E. J., Libby, V., Glatt, C. E. *et al.* (2011) "Transitional and translational studies of risk for anxiety." *Depression & Anxiety 28*(1), 18–28.

Chansky, T. E. (2004) *Freeing Your Child from Anxiety: Powerful, Practical Strategies to Overcome Your Child's Fears, Phobias, and Worries.* New York, NY: Broadway Books.

Ciarrochi, J. and Bailey, A. (2008) *A CBT Practitioner's Guide to ACT: How to Bridge the Gap between Cognitive Behavioral Therapy and Acceptance and Commitment Therapy.* Oakland, CA: New Harbinger Publications.

Codd III, R., Twohig, M. P., Crosby, J. M., and Enno, A. (2011) "Treatment of three anxiety disorder cases with acceptance and commitment therapy in a private practice." *Journal of Cognitive Psychotherapy 25*(3), 203–217.

Craske, M. G., Niles, A. N., Burklund, L. J., Wolitzky-Taylor, K. B., Vilardaga, J. P., Arch, J. J., & Lieberman, M. D. (2014). "Randomized Controlled Trial of Cognitive Behavioral Therapy and Acceptance and Commitment Therapy for Social Phobia: Outcomes and Moderators." *Journal Of Consulting And Clinical Psychology,* doi:10.1037/a0037212.

Cromer, B. (2011) "Adolescent Development." In: R. M. Kliegman, R. E. Behrman, H. B. Jenson, and B. F. Stanton (eds) *Nelson Textbook of Pediatrics.* 19th ed. Philadelphia, PA: Saunders Elsevier.

Erozkan, A. (2012) "Examination of relationship between anxiety sensitivity and parenting styles in adolescents." *Educational Sciences: Theory and Practice 12*(1), 52–57.

Fledderus, M., Bohlmeijer, E., Fox, J., Schreurs, K., and Spinhoven, P. (2013) "The role of psychological flexibility in a self-help acceptance and commitment therapy intervention for psychological distress in a randomized controlled trial." *Behaviour Research and Therapy 51*(3), 142–151.

Gatchel, R. J. and Rollings, K. H. (2008) "Therapy." *The Spine Journal 8*, 40–44.

Harris, R. (2009) *ACT Made Simple: An Easy-to-Read Primer on Acceptance and Commitment Therapy.* Oakland, CA: New Harbinger.

Hayes, S. C., Strosahl, K. D., & Wilson, K. G. (2012) *Acceptance and Commitment Therapy: The Process and Practice of Mindful Change* (2nd ed.). New York, NY, US: Guilford Press.

Hayes, S. C. (2005) *Get Out of Your Mind and Into Your Life: The New Acceptance and Commitment Therapy.* Oakland, CA: New Harbinger Publications.

Johnson, S., Blum, R., & Giedd, J. (2009) "Adolescent maturity and the brain: the promise and pitfalls of neuroscience research in adolescent health policy." *Journal of Adolescent Health*, 45(3), 216-221. doi:10.1016/j.jadohealth.2009.05.016

Kaufman, M. (2006) "Role of adolescent development in the transition process." *Progress in Transplantation, 16*(4), 286–290.

Kendall, P. C., Settipani, C. A., and Cummings, C. M. (2012). "No need to worry: The promising future of child anxiety research." *Journal of Clinical Child & Adolescent Psychology 41*(1), 103–115.

Kerns, C. M., Read, K. L., Klugman, J. and Philip, C. K. (2013). "Cognitive behavioral therapy for youth with social anxiety: Differential short and long-term treatment outcomes." *Journal of Anxiety Disorders 27*(2), 210–215.

Knowles, E. (2009) *Oxford dictionary of quotations* [electronic resource]. Edited by Elizabeth Knowles. Oxford, New York: Oxford University Press.

Lohmann, R. C. (2009) *The Anger Management Workbook for Teens.* Oakland, CA: New Harbinger Publications.

Low, N., Dugas, E., Karp, I., O'Loughlin, J., Constantin, E., and Rodriguez, D. (2012) "The association between parental history of diagnosed mood/anxiety disorders and psychiatric symptoms and disorders in young adult offspring." *BMC Psychiatry 12*(1), 1–8.

Luoma, J., Hayes, S. C., and Walser, R. D. (2007) *Learning ACT: An Acceptance and Commitment Therapy Skills-Training Manual for Therapists.* Oakland, CA: New Harbinger Publications.

Lusk, P. and Melnyk, B.M. (2013) "COPE for depressed and anxious teens: A brief cognitive-behavioral skills building intervention to increase access to timely, evidence-based treatment." *Journal of Child and Adolescent Psychiatric Nursing 26*(1), 23–31.

Meuret, A., Twohig, M., Rosenfield, D., Hayes, S., and Craske, M. (2012) "Brief acceptance and commitment therapy and exposure for panic disorder: A pilot study." *Cognitive and Behavioral Practice 19*(4), 606–618.

Partnership for a Drug-Free America (2008) "PDFA: Teens Using Drugs to Cope with Stress, Parents Underestimating Pressures." Available at www.drugfree.org, accessed on 12 November 2014.

Pharo, H., Sim, C., Graham, M., Gross, J., and Hayne, H. (2011) "Risky business: Executive function, personality, and reckless behavior during adolescence and emerging adulthood." *Behavioral Neuroscience 125*(6), 970–978.

Podell, J. L., Kendall, P. C., Gosch, E. A., Compton, S. N. *et al.* (2013) "Therapist factors and outcomes in CBT for anxiety in youth." *Professional Psychology: Research and Practice 44*(2), 89–98.

Reichenberg, L.W. (2014) *DSM-5 Essentials: The Savvy Clinician's Guide to the Changes in Criteria.* Hoboken, NJ: John Wiley & Sons, Inc.

Reid, T. (1786) *Essays on the Intellectual Powers of Man.* Charleston, NC: Nabu Press (2011 edition).

Reynolds, E., Schreiber, W., Geisel, K., MacPherson, L., Lejuez, C., and Ernst, M. (2013) "Influence of social stress on risk-taking behavior in adolescents." *Journal of Anxiety Disorders 27*(3), 272–277.

Rickwood, D. and Bradford, S. (2012) "The role of self-help in the treatment of mild anxiety in young people: An evidence-based review." *Psychology Research and Behavior Management 5*, 1–18.

Ridderinkhof, K. R., van den Wildenberg, W. M., Segalowitz, S. J., & Carter, C. S. (2004) "Neurocognitive mechanisms of cognitive control: The role of prefrontal cortex in action selection, response inhibition, performance monitoring, and reward-based learning." *Brain and Cognition*, 56(2), 129-140.

Saavedra, L. M., Silverman, W. K., Morgan-Lopez, A. A., and Kurtines, W. M. (2010) "Cognitive behavioral treatment for childhood anxiety disorders: Long-term effects on anxiety and secondary disorders in young adulthood." *Journal of Child Psychology & Psychiatry 51*(8), 924–934.

Shin, L. M., Rauch, S. L., and Pitman, R. K. (2006) "Amygdala, medial prefrontal cortex, and hippocampal function in PTSD." *Annals of the New York Academy of Sciences 1071*, 67–79.

Skinner, B. F. (1974) *About Behaviorism.* New York, NY: Knopf.

Sportel, B., de Hullu, E., de Jong, P. J., and Nauta, M. H. (2013) "Cognitive bias modification versus CBT in reducing adolescent social anxiety: A randomized controlled trial." *PLoS ONE 8*(5), 1–11.

Swain, J., Hancock, K., Hainsworth, C., and Bowman, J. (2013) "Acceptance and Commitment Therapy in the treatment of anxiety: A systematic review." *Clinical Psychology Review 33*(8), 965–978.

Swartz, J. R., Carrasco, M., Wiggins, J. L., Thomason, M. E., & Monk, C. S. (2014) "Age-related changes in the structure and function of prefrontal cortex–amygdala circuitry in children and adolescents: A multi-modal imaging approach." *Neuroimage*, 86212-220. doi:10.1016/j.neuroimage.2013.08.018

World Health Organization (2010). International classification of diseases (10th ed.) Available at www.who.int/classifications/icd/en, accessed on 12 November 2014.

RESOURCES

Suggested Reading

Bourne, E. (2005) *The Anxiety and Phobia Workbook*. 4th ed. Oakland, CA: New Harbinger Publications.

Brantley, J. (2007) *Calming Your Anxious Mind: How Mindfulness and Compassion Can Free You from Anxiety, Fear and Panic*. Oakland, CA: New Harbinger Publications.

Briers, S. (2012) *Brilliant Cognitive Behavioral Therapy: How to Use CBT to Improve your Mind and Your Life*. Harlow: Pearson.

Burns, D.D. (1990) *The Feeling Good Handbook*. New York, NY: Plume Book.

Forsyth, J. and Eifert, G. (2007) *The Mindfulness & Acceptance Workbook for Anxiety: A Guide to Breaking Free from Anxiety, Phobias & Worry Using Acceptance & Commitment Therapy*. Oakland, CA: New Harbinger Publications.

Harris, R. (2011) *The Confidence Gap: A Guide to Overcoming Fear and Self-Doubt*. Boston, MA: Trumpeter Books.

Online Resources

ACT Mindfully

Acceptance and Commitment Therapy (ACT) gets its name from one of its core messages: accept what is out of your personal control, and commit to action that improves and enriches your life.

www.actmindfully.com.au/acceptance_&_commitment_therapy

AnxietyBC

AnxietyBC provides self-help information and programs, as well as resources for parents and caregivers. Their mission is to increase awareness, promote education, and improve access to programs that work.

www.anxietybc.com

Anxiety and Depression Association of America—ADAA

ADAA is a national nonprofit organization dedicated to the prevention, treatment, and cure of anxiety, OCD, PTSD, depression, and related disorders and to improving the lives of all people who suffer from them.

www.adaa.org

Anxiety UK

Anxiety UK is a user-led organization run by individuals who have experienced anxiety. This organization is supported by a medical advisory panel.

www.anxietyuk.org.uk

Association for Contextual Behavioral Science

A worldwide online learning and research community, and a living resource for anyone interested in ACT, RFT, and Contextual Behavioral Science.

http://contextualscience.org

Beck Institute for Cognitive Behavior Therapy

Beck Institute for Cognitive Behavior Therapy is a leading international source for training, therapy, and resources in CBT.

www.beckinstitute.org

National Association of Cognitive-Behavioral Therapists

The NACBT is the leading organization dedicated exclusively to supporting, promoting, teaching, and developing Cognitive/Behavioral Therapy and those who practice it.

www.nacbt.org

National Institute of Mental Health—NIMH

The mission of NIMH is to transform the understanding and treatment of mental illnesses through basic and clinical research, paving the way for prevention, recovery, and cure.

www.nimh.nih.gov/health/topics/anxiety-disorders/index.shtml

The Association for Behavioral and Cognitive Therapies

The Association for Behavioral and Cognitive Therapies is an organization committed to the advancement of scientific approaches to the understanding and improvement of human functioning through the investigation and application of behavioral, cognitive, and other evidence-based principles to the assessment, prevention, treatment of human problems, and the enhancement of health and well-being.

www.abct.org/Home/?m=mAbout&fa=AboutABCT

The Albert Ellis Institute

AEI's therapeutic approach is based on rational emotive behavior therapy (REBT), a form of cognitive behavior therapy.

http://albertellis.org